ULTIMATE
JUMP ROPE
WORKOUTS

ULTIMATE JUMP ROPE WORKOUTS

WORKOUTS

Kick-Ass Programs to Strengthen Muscles,
Get Fit and Take Your Endurance to the Next Level

BRETT STEWART & JASON WARNER

Ulysses Press

Published in the United States by
Ulysses Press
P.O. Box 3440
Berkeley, CA 94703
www.ulyssespress.com

ISBN13: 978-1-61243-060-7
Library of Congress Control Number 2012937121

Printed in Canada by Webcom

10 9 8 7 6 5 4 3 2 1

Acquisitions Editor: Keith Riegert
Managing Editor: Claire Chun
Editor: Lily Chou
Proofreader: Elyce Berrigan-Dunlop
Cover design: what!design @ whatweb.com
Interior photographs: © Rapt Productions except page 25 © zimmytws/shutterstock.com (rhythm rope) and © Margoe Edwards/shutterstock.com (speed rope)
Cover photographs: © MichaelSvoboda/istockphoto.com
Models: Austin Akre, Mary J. Gines, Brett Stewart, Chad Taylor

Distributed by Publishers Group West

PLEASE NOTE: This book has been written and published strictly for informational purposes, and in no way should be used as a substitute for consultation with health care professionals. You should not consider educational material herein to be the practice of medicine or to replace consultation with a physician or other medical practitioner. The author and publisher are providing you with information in this work so that you can have the knowledge and can choose, at your own risk, to act on that knowledge. The author and publisher also urge all readers to be aware of their health status and to consult health care professionals before beginning any health program.

To JDub, Jase, Whitey or Jason—whatever moniker you go by—you changed my life with your help and support and I'm very proud to call you my friend and coauthor.

 —Brett

To my wife Anne-Marie, who supports whatever crazy thing I want to do.

 —Jason

CONTENTS

PART 1: OVERVIEW

Introduction

Endurance, fitness, flexibility, agility, strength, toning and cardiovascular training. These are the goals of almost any athlete—from professional sports figures to weekend warriors and everyone in between. Since improving fitness and athletic ability are at the top of the list for people all over the world, naturally they would make exercising a high priority in their lives, right?

Well, no. Real life is a lot more complicated than just following an exercise regimen in a book written by a couple guys who spend far too much time thinking about this stuff (hey, we resemble that statement!). Seriously, every day is busy enough without trying to fit in hours at the gym or on the treadmill. There has to be a better, more efficient way to get—and stay—fit!

Luckily, there is. With a simple, little piece of equipment and a 10- to 15-minute commitment three to five times a week, you can strengthen and tone your entire body while developing better endurance, flexibility, agility and core strength. You may be asking yourself, "What is this magic fitness tool? An AbBlaster 3000? A ThighRocker2k? Maybe it's a ThunderChair X11? All I know is I want one—at any price!"

Don't bother to get out your checkbook because this amazing fitness tool is a simple jump rope, as inexpensive as it is effective. Armed with a jump rope, you can perform dozens of exercises and routines like those found in this book to develop a fit, strong and ripped physique faster than you ever thought possible!

The only real investment you need to make is in yourself—committing to following the program and performing each workout with proper form, solid effort and high intensity. There are no "gimmies" in life. Whether you're on the golf course, at the big meeting or in the gym, success requires hard work and commitment. Getting fit is no exception. It'll require dedication and follow-through, but if you can find the fastest and most efficient way to boost your metabolism, endurance, agility and flexibility, that's the best way to go.

Most people who want to get fit fall into three different categories:

1. I want to get fit, but I just don't know how, I can't find a routine that I'll stick to and I don't have hours a day to spend at the gym.
2. I spend hours in the gym each week and am frustrated that I'm not getting the results I'm looking for.
3. I made positive gains for a while and now have hit a plateau. Should I begin learning a new routine and figuring out new exercises?

The programs here in *Ultimate Jump Rope Workouts* are designed to help with all of those fitness dilemmas and more. We've developed an easy-to-follow routine of physique-shredding and endurance-building activities coupled with exercises to target upper body, lower body and core strength to give you a full-body workout in just a fraction of the time it takes for you to find your membership card and drive to the gym.

Ultimate Jump Rope Workouts programs are short and intense and really work in reshaping your body and raising your fitness level. Best of all, they're extremely efficient. In as little as 10 minutes a day, three workouts per week, you can get a jumpstart on your fitness goals, break through plateaus and save hours at the gym (and hundreds in membership fees) in the process.

The Journey

The programs in this book were developed by Jason and Brett, two fitness and adventure junkies who've tackled just about everything, from Ironman triathlons to ultra-marathons, rugby to Tough Mudder and a whole lot of other crazy activities in between. These guys have been spotted racing cars across parking lots—by pushing them—and caught by a local news station in Arizona while working out in 110º heat.

We've been best friends for over a decade and teamed up on other fitness books: *7 Weeks to 50 Pull-Ups* and *7 Weeks to Getting Ripped* (a full-body workout built around bodyweight exercises, sprints and fitness games). Brett is an NCCPT Certified Personal Trainer and endurance maniac who can be found on top of a mountain or running a 100-mile race; he's 150 pounds soaking wet. Jason is an ISSA Certified Strength Trainer, competitive athlete and bodybuilding specialist. Putting on muscle is his specialty and, at 6 feet tall, he's a solid 65 pounds heavier than his coauthor. We couldn't be more different in size, shape, strength or endurance, yet we've created an easy-to-follow workout that we both enjoy and have used to raise our own fitness levels and that of many of our clients and training partners. Here's what got us here.

Jason's Story

My journey begins in freshman year of high school. I've just moved to a new town and enrolled in a new high school. A very typical high-school movie scenario ensues with just as much teen drama. The salient points are these:

#1. I'm 5'2" and 160 pounds. Trim, I am not.

#2. I meet my future wife (although I obviously didn't know that at the time), whom I immediately find stunning. She's 5'10" and 120 pounds. There's an 8-inch gap in my future.

#3. I'm quite the geek—computers, math, science, the whole lot.

I decide at some point during my freshman year that I'll work hard and get into great shape. I can't control my height, but I'll damn sure control my weight. I beg my mother for a home gym, a Nautilus band system of some sort. I rip

out an article from some magazine that was in the high school gym. I work at it, just like it says, for a period of months. Nothing.

Now the geek starts to kick in: more reading, learning, consuming of information than actual training. But this, I rationalize, is OK. After all, I need data!

By the end of my senior year, I've plotted and meandered my way to remaining 160 pounds, but I get lucky—nature throws me a bone and I grow to 5'10". I have an amazing amount of information sitting in my head but I haven't been able to successfully categorize, systematize and synthesize the information into a workable fitness protocol. But that, I learn in college, is because most of what I learned was junk. Garbage. Pseudo-information used to sell magazines, supplements or workout gear.

So how did I figure out everything I learned was WRONG? Easy. I found the fittest people I could and watched what they did, how they worked out, what they ate and which exercises they did and, more importantly, didn't do. I happened to be watching the Penn State football and basketball programs. Life-altering information.

I never saw an ab-roller, an elliptical machine or someone doing endless sets of curls to "peak" their biceps. Wind sprints, swimming, jumping rope and compound lifts—that's how elite athletes work out.

Since college, my fitness knowledge has exploded into other areas as well, including understanding nutrition better. One thing that has always been a constant, however, is the idea of doing it better with less. To get in great shape, to have a killer body and be unbelievably fit requires surprisingly little equipment.

Which leads me back to jumping rope. I love jumping rope. There are never any excuses with it. When I travel for work, I can always jump rope. When I'm on vacation with the wife and kids, I can jump rope. When I'm working 14 hours a day at the office, I can jump rope. It takes 10–20 minutes to get a killer workout and I literally need no equipment (I can just shadow jump if I don't have any of my ropes).

My fitness journey isn't complete. I'm sure I'll learn more and adapt my training, nutrition and lifestyle as more information becomes available, but I know this more than anything: Jumping rope will always be a part of my routine. The benefits are just too great to ignore.

Brett's Story

Like Jason, I was in no way a "fit" kid. I was usually second-to-last picked in recess games, but only if the last kid was on crutches. Nothing says "athletic prowess" (or lack thereof) like being last up to the plate in kickball behind all the girls, yet I somehow managed to hit a new low every year when the Presidential Physical Fitness Test came along. I was the pudgy kid who couldn't even do one pull-up and my physical education teacher could usually count the number of push-ups and sit-ups I completed on one hand. Needless to say, I was the butt of quite a few jokes in T-ball when I was exhausted from simply running to first base.

As the chubby kid, there were no real expectations for me to be good at sports and I didn't put much of an effort into trying to improve. Soccer, baseball, basketball and most other sports were just a way to pass the time. I knew there was no way I was getting the game-winning hit in Little League or making the game-winning shot in basketball—most games I never even got passed the ball. Honestly, I just gave up and figured I'd never be fit like a lot of the other kids in my teams. I always dreamed of being in shape, but I lacked the motivation to put in the effort to change my eating and exercise habits.

Fast forward to my early 30s. That kid grew into a 30-pounds-overweight smoker who got winded climbing up a flight of stairs. I nearly died from exhaustion during a pick-up basketball game with my new co-worker Jason. He was about four inches taller than me but it might as well have been a foot since I was slow, had no endurance and couldn't shoot a basketball to save my life. Even though he destroyed me that game, a friendship was born and my competitive fire was stoked. I knew if I could just get into shape and lose 20 or 30 pounds, I could beat him. Little did I know that friendship would change my life—as well as my fitness—and usher in some of the best years of my life. My wife, my career and this very book are all the results of the game played on the basketball court that day, and I have my buddy JDub to thank for inspiring me to get fit.

Thanks to this book, you have your own JDub and Brett to encourage you to get fit. Don't believe it? You can contact us directly at www.7weekstofitness.com with any questions or comments. You can also get tips, tricks and additional programs directly from us to help you get fit.

About the Book

Ultimate Jump Rope Workouts is about jumping rope. Very simple. But more than that, this book is about learning the proper way to jump rope and using these skills to get into great shape. It's also about showcasing a fantastic and often-overlooked exercise for lifelong fitness.

This book is about getting better, being better and changing for the better. We just happen to talk quite a bit about jumping rope to get you there. Along with the jump rope techniques, we also add a dozen different exercises to strengthen and tone your entire body and give you a well-rounded program for total-body fitness. Once you feel the burn of a high-intensity jump rope–based circuit, most other exercises will feel like a walk in the park.

Part 1 explains the benefits of using a progressive, high-intensity training program based around jump rope techniques and details how anyone at any fitness level can lose weight and get fit quickly. It also gives you tips on picking the perfect rope and other gear you'll need.

Part 2 introduces proper jump rope form in addition to the progressive Prep, Basic and Advanced programs, each featuring multiple jump rope–based moves as well as several unique exercises to strengthen your entire body, develop lasting endurance and get you fit.

Part 3 features photographs and descriptions of all the jumps to get you started quickly. It also has guidelines for building your own jump rope–based workouts.

Appendix lays out warm-ups, stretches and additional exercises for a well-rounded workout.

Jumping Rope Is Better Than...

Jumping rope is one of the top calorie burners on the planet, ranking up there in calories burned per minute with a vigorous basketball game, a six-minute-mile run and a 20-miles-per-hour bike ride. Aside from the calories-burned-per-minute argument, there's the equipment. Swimming needs a pool, cycling needs a bike and a road and running simply needs shoes and time (not to mention few people can run six-minute miles for very long). Jumping rope needs a rope and about four feet of horizontal space and eight feet of vertical space. Essentially, anywhere you can stand, you can jump rope.

Additionally, jumping rope can be used as a high-intensity interval training (HIIT) workout. HIIT is an exercise strategy used to improve athletic performance, burn fat and increase cardiovascular fitness. The sessions tend to be short, ranging from 5–20 minutes, and involve intensely focused work. How focused? How intense? Typically they're anywhere from 75% to 100% max effort for the allotted work time. But don't confuse short in duration with easy. There's nothing easy about HIIT training. In fact, highly trained athletes typically turn to HIIT to boost their performance when traditional methods fail. HIIT is no joke—the fact that jumping rope, with its minimal space and equipment needs, can be used to get a killer workout in a short amount of time makes it a winner.

When advised to take up jumping rope, people typically ask, "What about X?" or "How does that compare to Y?" This is expected. Humans by nature are comparative and like to categorize and compare against known situations. So how does jumping rope compare to some of the most common exercises out there? I'm glad you asked!

NOT JUST FOR LITTLE GIRLS

Says Jason, "I've been using jump rope as an integral part of my fitness program since college, when I first started to get serious about fitness. It was five seconds after I picked up my first jump rope when I realized the benefit, and 10 seconds after that when someone scoffed and asked me for the first time, 'Why are you jumping rope? Are you a 10-year-old girl?' I still occasionally get that question now when I jump rope.

"I travel with a jump rope. I've jumped rope in airports, in hotels, in stairwells, in the garage, in the basement, in my bedroom, on the porch. Heck, I shadow jumped (jumping without a jump rope, see page 58) in airplanes! Bottom line, jumping rope leaves me with very little excuses and I like that.

"There are other benefits as well. I developed patellofemoral pain and tendinitis in both my knees from years of running. I partially tore my right Achilles tendon while training for basketball. If I do too much running, my Achilles and knees ache for days. If I cycle too much, my knees act up. Jumping rope, while not low impact, is what I call limited impact and I get a workout that's absolutely killer with minimum stress on my body. I can go out and grind out an hour run at seven- to eight-minute miles, or I can jump rope for 10 minutes and reap the same cardiovascular benefits."

If jumping rope were an investment, it'd be a definite "buy." The effectiveness, the calories burned per minute and the lack of equipment needed makes it great exercise. When compared to its contemporaries, jumping rope not only holds its own, it shines. Searching for an extremely effective calorie-burning exercise? Look no further.

ACTIVITY	CALORIES BURNED	EQUIPMENT	EFFECTIVENESS
Jumping Rope (basic fast)	14 calories/minute	Jump Rope	A+
Swimming (75 yards/minute)	12 calories/minute	Pool	A+
Running (8 mph)	15 calories/minute	Shoes, Road/Treadmill	A
Cycling (16–19 mph)	14 calories/minute	Bike/Stationary Bike	A
Basketball (game)	9 calories/minute	Court, Friends	B
Soccer (game)	11 calories/minute	Field, Friends	B
Calisthenics (intense)	9 calories/minute	Class, DVD	C

Frequently Asked Questions

Jumping rope? Seriously? Like double dutch? An odd first question, to be sure. And, yes—jumping rope. However, this program is most probably not like any jumping rope you've done before. We'll be pushing you to your limits until you ask us to back off, and we will, for a split second, before we push you even further. Jumping rope is a fantastic all-around workout, one that's near the top of the calories-burned-per-minute graph. In fact, it ranks at the top of the charts in calories burned per minute.

Q. Shouldn't I just run?

A. Running is a great way to build cardio-vascular endurance and improve overall physical fitness. If you can run and enjoy it, by all means do. However, many people can't run, don't like to run or simply don't have the time to run. Jumping rope is an alternative that has advantages over running. Namely, it can be done in less time, in a smaller space and with less impact on the body. All these combined mean that jumping rope is a great way to get and stay in shape.

Q. I can't jump rope!

A. We beg to differ! You can't jump rope *yet*. Jumping rope is a skill and, just like any other skill, it takes practice. If you haven't jumped rope in a while (or ever), it'll take some time and could even be frustrating, but over the course of a couple of days or possibly up to a week, you'll get the hang of it. And then you'll only get better and have more fun. In the meantime, there's always shadow jumping (see page 58)!

Q. Do I have to jump rope for hours?

A. Jumping rope is more like sprinting than jogging. You'll never catch a sprinter running sprints for hours and you won't find us advocating that for jump rope either. We'll build you up to multiple minutes—as many as tens of minutes—of jumping rope, but nothing approaching hours. Rather than extend the workout by time, we're going to play with intensity. Intensity is the key to getting a great workout. Jumping rope allows us to raise and lower intensity like a dial by manipulating various aspects of the workout, including jumping speed, height, travel distance and the

number of swings before your feet touch the ground (see Double Unders on page 72). You'll get an amazing workout in a short amount of time.

Q. Will I be able to get a six pack by jumping rope?

A. We have a saying: "Abs are made in the kitchen," meaning that most people would benefit more from changes in diet if they hope to achieve a six pack. However, the 80/20 rule is in effect: If diet affects 80% of your six-pack appearance, the other 20% is all about workout and energy expenditure.

Jumping rope will not only help that, it'll jumpstart it. Jumping rope burns a high amount of calories per minute. It's also a high-intensity workout that keeps your metabolism high throughout the day. As I mentioned earlier, jumping rope has more in common with sprinting that it does jogging. These intense workouts combined with upper-body, core and lower-body exercises will put you on the fast track to six-pack abs.

Q. My primary sport is X. Will jumping rope help me be better at that sport?

A. Yes. We want to leave the answer at just "yes" and move on, but we should explain. There isn't a sport in the world that wouldn't be helped by its participants jumping rope. Let's look at some of the benefits of jumping rope:

- Explosive power
- Muscular endurance
- Coordination
- Cardiovascular fitness
- Mental focus
- Proprioception
- Balance

It should be obvious by this list that jumping rope would benefit any sport, from basketball, football and soccer to hiking, swimming and cycling. Jumping rope is a great way to get and stay in shape, not to mention cross-train and develop skills needed for daily life. Whether you're training for a marathon or racing motocross, you've picked up the right book to help improve your fitness, flexibility, endurance and strength.

New to Jumping Rope? Start Here

Here are two common complaints about jumping rope from people starting out: It's for kids (aka, not cool) and they don't have the coordination for it. We can't help you with the cool factor, although we'd argue that Muhammad Ali, Mike Tyson, Evander Holyfield and every other boxer in history might have something to say about that. But, if someone doesn't want to jump rope because of a perceived "uncoolness," all we can say is that's their loss. Us? We're going to use it no matter what others think because we're doing this for ourselves, to get a great workout and to be in the best shape we can be all the time.

The second complaint, coordination, is a more real issue, but one just as easily overcome. Most people think they need to be doing fancy tricks, jumping all over the place and generally being acrobatic, to "jump rope." Nothing could be further from the truth. The base jump, two feet, single rope pass, moderate pace, is so utterly effective that if you never veered from this move alone, you'd get a tremendous physique.

However, the fact remains that people think this is a problem and our advice to them is to start simple. Start by shadow jumping. Progress to several jumps, working your way up to 30 seconds of continuous jumping. Once you hit 30 seconds, start to count your individual jumps and work your way to 200 continuous jumps. You'll get there surprisingly fast.

We have to admit to some trickery when broaching the subject with people. We tend to simply advise someone to stick with shadow jumping...forever. Shadow jumping is a GREAT workout and you can achieve a great deal just doing this. Why is this a trick? Well, most people tend to do this for a time, get comfortable with the motions, build a bit of strength in their base and then want something more. They want to use an actual jump rope. Usually by the time someone picks up a jump rope after shadow jumping for several weeks, it takes only minutes for them to be jumping away at a pretty decent rate. This is an example of a bit of human competitive nature at work.

Shadow Jumping

As mentioned earlier, shadow jumping is an incredibly effective alternative to jumping rope. It's also a great transition to actually jumping rope. If there's any question about your ability to jump rope, if you don't have a jump rope or you find yourself in a situation where you can't use a jump rope (did we mention that Jason does this on planes?), shadow jumping is great.

What's shadow jumping? Simply, shadow jumping is jumping rope without the rope. You mimic the exact movements of jumping rope but without holding the jump rope. This means you stand erect with your hands to your side as you would with a jump rope, keeping your shoulders back and head up. You jump on the balls of your feet and move your wrists in a circular motion, just as you would with a jump rope. Go ahead and try it now. Just do two or three and you'll see it in action.

When shadow jumping, you do everything exactly as you would with a jump rope, which also means you can do all the same exercises and jumps that you could with a jump rope. This

makes it incredibly effective and simple to get a workout no matter the time or situation.

Jason loves shadow jumping. When traveling, he'll do it not only on the plane, but in his hotel room, in stairwells and even in the men's room in airports (too much information?).

Picking the Right Jump Rope

Nothing makes jumping rope less fun than having the wrong size rope. Too short and you're always catching your feet. Too long and you have an unwieldy weapon akin to a whip bouncing off the ground and smacking you in the shins. Either way, you have a rather unenjoyable experience. That's why picking a proper jump rope length is important. Luckily, it's easy to do.

ROPE LENGTH

How can you tell if the jump rope you already have or see in the store is the right length? Take a jump rope and stand with both feet in the

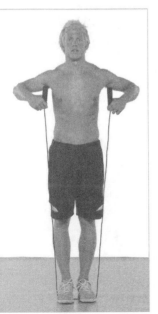

middle. Now take the handles and put them up to your armpits. It's the proper length if the handles are roughly in the same area as your armpits, give or take an inch. If the handles are over your shoulders or below your chest, you obviously have the wrong size.

But what if you want to order a new, fancy jump rope online

and you don't know your height? There are two methods.

QUICK AND DIRTY   This method seems to work 85% of the time and works well if you don't have any longer- or shorter-than-average extremities. If you're looking for an extremely accurate method to finding the ideal jump rope, skip to the next section.

HEIGHT	ROPE LENGTH
Under 5'6" (under 168 cm)	8 feet
5'6"–5'11" (168–80 cm)	9 feet
6'–6'5" (193–96 cm)	10 feet
Over 6'5" (over 196 cm)	11 feet

MORE ACCURATE   This method will simulate the jump rope to give you the length you need. Using a string, piece of rope or other rope-like entity, you'll do the same thing above to determine if the length is right: Stand in the middle of the string and bring the ends to either armpit. Mark or note the point on the string that was roughly at your armpit. Measure the distance between those two points and you'll have the length.

Now, most people aren't going to get a clean foot marker and since jump ropes tend to come in 1-foot increments between 8 feet and 11 feet, just use your judgment. If your string measures 7'8", obviously 8 feet is going to be safer than 7 feet. First-grade math skills of rounding up come in to play.

ROPE STYLE

Choosing a jump rope style is also important. The rope you choose depends on your goals and, more importantly, where you'll be jumping.

NOT QUITE RIGHT

If you find yourself with a rope that's too short, it's time to take a trip back to the store to exchange it for a longer one. Attempting to jump with a rope that's too short will cause you to hunch over and perform each jump with improper form. Worse yet, the chances of tripping yourself and landing in a subsequent faceplant increase dramatically.

If you have a rope that's a little too long, you can adjust it by looping the rope around your hand to take up some of the slack. This is a short-term solution, however—if you plan on using a rope for this entire program, you really should get one that's the proper length for you.

A rhythm rope is very good for jump rope novices as it allows you to find your jumping rhythm more easily, as the name implies. Experienced jumpers who plan to jump mostly outside on pavement, concrete or other very hard surfaces will find a rhythm rope most suitable.

If you plan to jump inside, on mats or padding, a speed rope is more appropriate. It's also what you'll need if you want to do some of the more advanced moves (like the Double Under).

RHYTHM ROPE We love rhythm ropes. We reach for this rope when we're just looking to get a steady cardio workout. It's nothing fancy and there's nothing too difficult about it. It's just a great workout with no fuss.

What makes the rhythm rope unique is that the actual rope, typically nylon, is wrapped in hard plastic beads. The beads make the rope very durable for use on harsh surfaces such as asphalt or concrete. The beads also add heft and weight to the rope, subsequently making it much easier to wield. As you jump, the added weight of the beads creates a smooth arc and natural cadence to the jumps. One jump is practically indistinguishable from the previous or next, making for a very consistent jumping experience. It's just what you want when you're starting out or want to get a steady cardio session in.

SPEED ROPE The speed rope, which is what boxers typically use, is another beast entirely. We like to think of the speed rope as an ankle whip with two handles for better leverage.

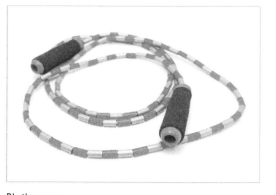

Rhythm rope

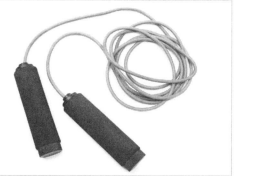

Speed rope

Put bluntly, missing a jump and smacking your shins with this thing will hurt (did we mention you should get a properly sized jump rope?).

Is that all? They hurt? Great. No way! No one would use them if they didn't have a huge upside as well. The thing about speed ropes is that you can go fast—like lightning quick. Watch an experienced boxer jump rope and you'll be amazed at what can be done. We're constantly in awe of some of the things we see other people do with the speed rope. By comparison, we're just pretty boring amateurs trying to get a great workout.

Back to the speed rope: It's typically a nylon or malleable plastic cord with great action in the handles. They're typically quite light and really whip up the wind noise as you jump. We use it when we're looking to bust our butts and completely drain ourselves—we crank out a couple hundred in the shortest amount of time possible, mixing in some Double Unders. Talk about working up a sweat in under five minutes!

Before You Begin

In order to focus on completing this program successfully, it's important that you're ready for the challenge and know your limits. When you begin any new exercise program, it's imperative that you talk with your doctor first and make sure you're healthy enough to participate in physical strength training and conditioning.

Despite jumping rope's reputation as a children's activity, it's quite physically strenuous. As the programs also feature full-body calisthenics, it's extremely important that you take into consideration any previous injuries or musculature imbalances and start slowly, performing each exercise with proper form. Take the proper warm-up and post-exercise stretching seriously (see page 84). You should

warm up for 5–10 minutes, perform your workout, and then stretch for 5–10 minutes. (We've included a few warm-up exercises and stretches that specifically target the muscles used in each workout.)

Most importantly, perform each workout at a pace that you can handle while you build up your strength and stamina. You can't rush progress—take your time and you'll see the results.

Jumping rope is uniquely challenging for various body parts, including the feet, ankles, calves, hamstrings, glutes and hips (the entire lower body) as well as the wrists and shoulders. A sure-fire way to knock yourself off the program is to push yourself too hard during the first few workouts. It's all too common for athletes of all abilities to start a new program and develop delayed onset muscle soreness (DOMS) as soon as 5 and as long as 72 hours after intense exercise. The best advice for any individual starting any new exercise regimen is to take it slowly. The first week is all about acclimating yourself to the routine; there's plenty of time to push yourself as you progress through the program. Feel free to take additional rest or call it a day if you feel you're overdoing it.

Soreness when starting a new exercise routine is natural, but if it persists for multiple days or inhibits natural activities, take an additional day of rest. If the soreness continues or you have any sharp pains, discontinue the workout and consult a physician right away.

PART 2: ULTIMATE JUMP ROPE WORKOUTS

The Workouts

So far we've discussed the whys of jumping rope. Now we'll get into the how and the what. We'll start by talking about the actual mechanism of jumping, swinging and landing and then cover the three comprehensive programs (Prep, Basic and Advanced) in depth.

Each program was created specifically to include core and upper- and lower-body exercises along with extreme jump rope training to maximize your fat-burning, strength-building and endurance development. These efficient programs are designed to take no more than 15 minutes a day (including warm-up and cool-down) in order to transform your fitness as rapidly as possible. For the best results, use the descriptions below to decide which level is best for you.

For those new to jump rope training or getting back into fitness after extended time off, the Prep Program on page 38 would be the best place to start. The Prep Program is based around learning the basics of jumping rope and developing proper form for the basic bodyweight exercises you'll be performing throughout the programs. It gently ramps you up, building the necessary base in both endurance, flexibility and strength. Remember, putting stress on your tendons and ligaments without strengthening them first will make you more likely to experience an injury. The way to avoid this is to slowly build up your fitness and let your body adapt. Don't make the common rookie mistake that takes you out of training for a significant period of time—and that's by overdoing it!

Athletes who've been jumping rope for less than six months should feel comfortable starting with the Basic Program (page 43), the "meat and potatoes" of the book. Using easy and intermediate jumps along with tried-and-true calisthenics, this four-week intermediate program is built around an exercise routine that's accessible to fitness enthusiasts of nearly every level, whether you're looking to raise your fitness to new levels, shake up a stale exercise routine or maintain a high level of fitness after you've completed any of the programs. Each individual set improves strength and endurance through supersets to develop your body in as little time as possible. It's an excellent all-around program to use any time of the year, any time in your training. If you're an athlete who wants to break out of your normal gym routine to enhance cardiovascular endurance and gain a lean physique, the Basic Program is the place to start.

The experienced jumper who feels confident performing 200 consecutive jumps at a reasonable pace should be ready to jump up (I couldn't resist) to the Advanced Program on page 48. The Advanced Program is extreme, featuring high-intensity interval training (HIIT) and supersets to build extreme strength and stamina and develop total-body fitness. You won't find many "easy" jumps in this level and, by shortening the rest periods, this program is designed to really push the pace. The extreme jumps combined with bodyweight exercises aren't for the faint of heart and should be approached with a bit of humility. This program is called "advanced" for a reason! Do you want to rapidly develop your best physique ever in the shortest possible amount of time? When you're ready, the Advanced Program is here for you.

Keep in mind that the jumps used in this book are just a small subset of jumps out there in the jump rope world. There

NOTE FOR THOSE RECOVERING FROM INJURY

The Prep Program is a must! Don't jump into a more advanced program and risk injury! The Prep Program is quick (four weeks) and you'll give your body time to acclimate, recover and build a solid base for the Basic and Advanced programs.

are literally hundreds of jumps, some very acrobatic. If you feel adventurous enough and are so inclined, you can take the routines in an entirely new direction by enhancing them with these new jumps. We keep a curated list of some of the best jumps on our website, www.7weekstofitness.com.

A Word about Intensity

The higher the level of intensity you put into the workout, the more you'll reap the fat-burning, strength-building and endurance-developing benefits. On paper, the difference in jumping 70 times a minute to 100 doesn't seem as significant as it is in practice. Without question you'll achieve maximum results the harder you push yourself. The goal of a high-intensity workout is to alternate between performing an exercise at a "comfortable" level and at an "all-out" effort for a specific duration.

How do you determine what's comfortable vs. what's all-out without falling for the common mistake of over- or under-estimating your exertion level? Unfortunately, there's no magic number: These rates are relative to each individual and they change from workout to workout. Quite often novice athletes perceive their effort to be 90% when, in fact, it's closer to 60%. As you become more attuned to your body by progressing through the workouts, you should have a better understanding about how you feel during different levels of exertion, but even for seasoned athletes it's sometimes difficult to pinpoint accurately. Heart rate monitors surely help if you're the type who appreciates data, but some athletes would rather determine their output based on feel.

Here are some examples of what each of these exertion levels should feel like:

Comfortable Exertion

- You should be able to hold a conversation with a training partner or sing along to a song without being out of breath.
- Breathing should be rhythmic and controlled, you should be breathing deeply and not gasping for air.
- Your heart rate should be around 50–60% of your maximum. (See "Finding Your Target Heart Rate" on page 31)
- For most individuals, setting a treadmill on "5" would be consistent with this level of effort.

All-Out /Maximal Effort

- Talking would be limited to one-word responses between you and a training partner. Forget singing along to a song—you most likely won't even be able to remember the words.
- Breathing is rapid and ever-increasing throughout the interval's duration. This is clearly not a pace that you can continue for an extended period of time.
- Your heart rate should top out between 90–95% of your maximum.
- For most individuals, this would be a 9 or 10 on a treadmill.

Because HIIT intervals require short, intense bursts of maximal effort, it's vital to give "that little bit extra"—no holding back, nothing left in the tank. You don't need to save it for the last mile, the last minute of the game or running back home. THIS IS IT! This is the home stretch, the last minute of the game. Push your limits during this workout and you'll be rewarded by developing a better physique,

FINDING YOUR TARGET HEART RATE

In order to optimize fat burning, it's important for you to calculate your resting heart rate (RHR) and use that to find your target heart rate (THR).

To calculate your maximum heart rate (MHR) (the theoretical maximum beats per minute your heart can physically handle):

$$220 - \text{YOUR AGE} = \text{MHR}$$

To calculate 60% of your MHR to keep your cardio in the fat-burning zone (or THR):

$$220 - \text{YOUR AGE} \times \text{DESIRED \%} = \text{THR}$$

In order to make your THR percentage even more accurate, you need to know your resting heart rate (RHR). Take your HR first thing in the morning when you wake up and use this formula:

$$(220 - \text{YOUR AGE} - \text{RHR}) \times \text{DESIRED \%} + \text{RHR} = \text{THR} \quad \textit{140}$$

Note that you subtract your RHR before multiplying by the desired HR% and then add your RHR back in.

improved athletic performance and increased cardiovascular endurance.

After each maximal effort you'll be rewarded with a period of comfortable exertion to recover, hydrate and catch your breath. During this period it's very important that you take it easy and allow your heart rate to return to less elevated levels. This could be as low as 50% (if you recover quickly) to around 70% for most people. If your heart rate doesn't return to below 75% during your minimal exertion period, you need to extend your rest or stop exercising until it does.

High-intensity training is not without its dangers. You're stressing your heart and lungs along with the rest of your body to perform exercises at a rapid cadence. As we covered in "Before You Begin" (page 26), it's extremely important that you seek a doctor's clearance before attempting this—or any—exercise program.

Build Your Own Routine

Most people are going to see no reason to do anything past the programs outlined in this book, and with good reason. The jump rope and exercise programs presented here are complete and taxing enough for most individuals.

However, if you find yourself wanting more or you tire of these programs for any reason, we encourage you to make your own. Our advice is to experiment with jumps, time and rest. Those three elements are what make a workout and program succeed or fail. Obviously the harder the jump, the shorter the jumping period might need to be with a longer rest period. However, pushing yourself to go harder, longer and with shorter rest will make the overall workout that much more challenging, working you harder and getting you into better shape. Check www.7weekstofitness.com for some ideas.

Basics of Jumping

Part of the beauty about jumping rope is its simplicity. If you have a rope and enough room to swing it, you can get a workout. The rest of the picture is the form that's used when jumping said rope, and that can be a sight to behold when the rope is in talented hands. In this section we'll cover the basics, from how to hold the rope through the swing, body position, jump and, finally, the landing. It's pretty simple— millions of children do it every day. Now, if we can just get more adults to join them, we'd all be much fitter!

The Grip

Hold the jump rope handles loosely with the rope coming out between your thumb and forefinger. Use just enough pressure to not let the handles fall from your hands. Your arms should be at your sides, hip level, and elbows bent approximately 45 degrees away from your body. The goal is going to be speed, which means you need to be loose. You'll want to stay this way as you jump and keeping a good grip—not too tight, not too loose—on the handles will be crucial.

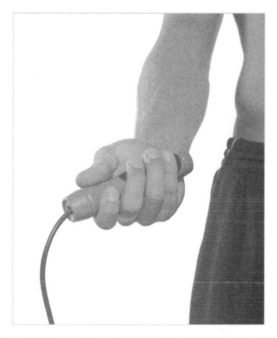

Proper grip: Loose but with just enough pressure to not let the handles fall from your hands

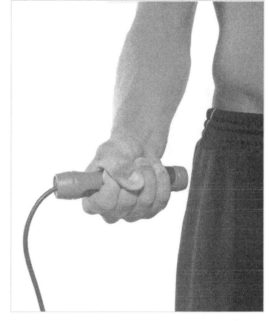

Improper grip: Too tight; creates unnecessary tension in the arms

The Swing

The swing is typically the component people fear the most, but it's really the least important element to the entire movement. The swing is really a reaction to how fast you're rotating your wrists. There isn't much to the swing other than physics.

Even so, we'll walk through a good way to get comfortable with the swing.

1 Start with a handle in each hand and the rope behind you at your heels.

2 Swing the rope over your head easily (don't swing hard here—we're just getting the hang of the swing) and let it hit the ground just in front of your toes. Your upper arms shouldn't move during this motion. The initiation of the swing and the swing speed should come from circular forearm and wrist motion.

3 – 4 The rope will hit the ground and then your legs. Step over the rope with both feet to get back to the starting position (rope behind your heels).

Congratulations! That's your first jump! Now do it again. Now once more. How does it feel? Keep doing this until it feels painfully, almost embarrassingly simple. Once you get to that point, we can move on to jumping and landing.

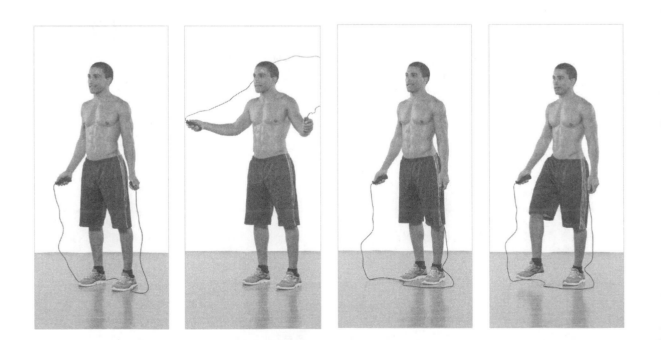

Body Position

Most people think of jumping rope as "hard on the joints." Nothing could be further from the truth. With proper footwork, body positioning and good take-off and landing, jumping rope is actually very easy on the joints. The thing is, most people don't jump properly!

Here's you checklist for correct body position:

• Stand upright with your head squarely between your shoulders and your eyes looking straight ahead, not up or down. It's important to keep your eyes focused horizontally. Doing this keeps your head level, and having a level head keeps your torso aligned properly throughout the jump. Put another way, your body will follow your eyes and head. If you have your head back and looking up, you'll have too much back bend. If your head is down, looking at your feet or the ground, you'll have too much forward torso lean. Both of these are suboptimal and can lead to injury.

• Your feet are at most shoulder-width apart but at least three inches apart. Contrary to popular belief, your feet should not be locked together. Having slight separation between them is proper form and allows for the jumps we'll outline later in the book.

• Have your weight slightly forward on the balls of your feet. Your knees will naturally bend to keep your upright posture. The slight knee bend offers the cushioning so crucial to healthy jump roping. Keep the slight knee

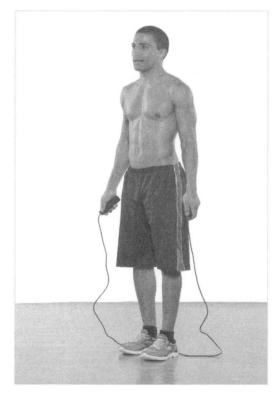
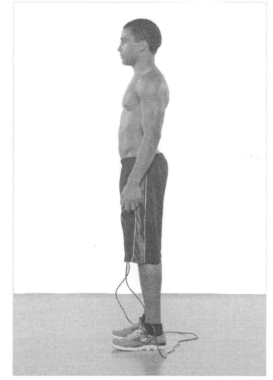

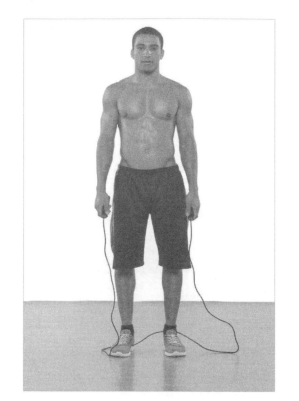

bend throughout the jumps. In addition, NEVER jump or land on a locked-out joint. Imagine if your knees were locked and your leg was essentially straight as you jumped and landed. The sheering forces of a simple jump are estimated to be six times your body weight. If you legs are locked out, nature's shock absorbers (your muscles) can't do anything to stop the force from radiating through your body.

• Your abdominals, glutes and hips (your core) should all be engaged, meaning you're aware of them and have slight tension in them. Your core is the engine that makes twisting, jumping and general movement possible. Having a weak core leads to many, many problems, including knee, ankle, back and hip pain. Actively engaging your core does two things: It acts to engage your core and prepare it for work (you want your core involved in the jumps, offering cushioning and thus reducing the risk of injury). It also increases the work of your core, thus strengthening your core and further reducing the risk of injury. This is one cycle you WANT. Keep your core engaged and reap the benefits of a healthier body and less pain everywhere.

These reasons are why it's crucial to use correct body position.

The Jump & the Landing

Once you have the correct body position, actually jumping and landing is a simple matter of engaging your muscles and firing them. Sounds simple enough, right?

THE JUMP

1 Lean slightly forward, with your weight approximately 80% on your forefoot. Engage your shoulders and abdomen (you want a stable trunk).

2 Once they're engaged, keep a slight bend in your hips and knees as you mentally "flick" or "kick" your toes down like you're trying to push the ground away from you.

Congratulations—that was your first jump!

THE LANDING

1 Keep the slight bend in your hips. As your forefoot touches down, let your knees bend slightly as your legs absorb the landing. At this stage, you should essentially be back in the starting position for the jump, coiled and ready to repeat the jump.

POINTERS TO JUMPING AND LANDING

1. Always jump and land on the balls of your feet.
2. There should be a slight bend in your hips/waist, knees and ankles as you both jump and land. You should NEVER jump or land on a locked-out joint.
3. Keep your shoulders slightly back.
4. Keep your head looking straight ahead, eyes focused horizontally.

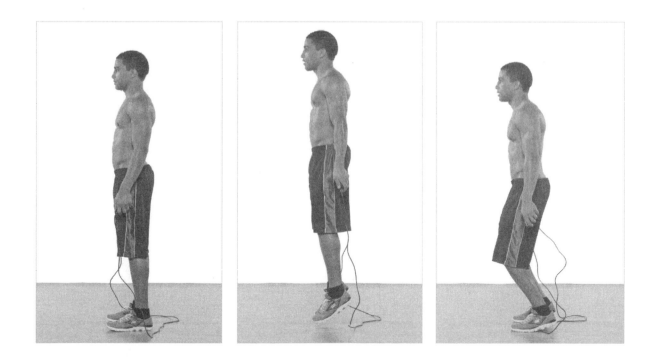

Prep Program

Use this program if you've been sedentary for quite some time, are new to jump rope or want a gentle introduction to the programs outlined in the rest of the book. This level is great to help your body adjust to the increased demands we'll place on it in the follow-up programs.

Prep WEEK 1

Note: Rest and recovery are vital to the success of the programs and should be included as prescribed on the schedules. Remember also to warm up before your workout and stretch afterward! See pages 84–92 for ideas.

MON	TUE	WED	THU	FRI	SAT	SUN
:30 Basic Jump (p60)		:30 Basic Jump (p60)		1:00 Basic Jump (p60)		
:30 Rest		:30 Rest		:30 Rest		
:30 Basic Jump (p60)		1:00 Basic Jump (p60)		1:30 Basic Jump (p60)		
:30 Rest		:30 Rest		:30 Rest		
1:00 Basic Jump (p60)		1:00 Basic Jump (p60)		1:30 Basic Jump (p60)		
:30 Rest	Rest	:30 Rest	Rest	:30 Rest	Rest	Rest
10 Side Hops (p95)		12 Marching Twists (p104)		10 Forward Jumps (p96)		
:30 Rest		:30 Rest		:30 Rest		
1:00 Basic Jump (p60)		1:30 Basic Jump (p60)		2:00 Basic Jump (p60)		
:30 Rest		:30 Rest		:30 Rest		
1:00 Basic Jump (p60)		2:00 Basic Jump (p60)		2:00 Basic Jump (p60)		
8 Reverse Crunches (p98)		8 Cobras (p99)		8 Wood Chops (p99)		

Prep   WEEK 2

Note: Rest and recovery are vital to the success of the programs and should be included as prescribed on the schedules. Remember also to warm up before your workout and stretch afterward! See pages 84–92 for ideas.

MON	TUE	WED	THU	FRI	SAT	SUN
:30 Basic Jump (p60)		1:00 Basic Jump (p60)		1:00 Basic Jump (p60)		
:30 Rest		:30 Rest		:30 Rest		
:30 Skier Jump (p62)		1:00 Skier Jump (p62)		1:00 Skier Jump (p62)		
:30 Rest		:30 Rest		:30 Rest		
1:30 Basic Jump (p60)		1:30 Basic Jump (p60)		2:00 Basic Jump (p60)		
:30 Rest		:30 Rest		:30 Rest		
10 Wood Chops (p99)	Rest	10 Side Hops (p95)	Rest	12 Forward Jumps (p96)	Rest	Rest
:30 Rest		:30 Rest		:30 Rest		
1:30 Basic Jump (p60)		2:00 Basic Jump (p60)		2:30 Basic Jump (p60)		
:30 Rest		:30 Rest		:30 Rest		
2:30 Basic Jump (p60)		3:00 Basic Jump (p60)		3:30 Basic Jump (p60)		
10 Hip Raises (p100)		12 Bird Dogs (p101)		10 Reverse Crunches (p98)		

Prep WEEK 3

Note: Rest and recovery are vital to the success of the programs and should be included as prescribed on the schedules. Remember also to warm up before your workout and stretch afterward! See pages 84–92 for ideas.

MON	TUE	WED	THU	FRI	SAT	SUN
1:00 Basic Jump (p60)		1:00 Basic Jump (p60)		1:00 Basic Jump (p60)		
:30 Rest		:30 Rest		:30 Rest		
1:00 Skier Jump (p62)		1:00 Skier Jump (p62)		2:00 Skier Jump (p62)		
:30 Rest		:30 Rest		:30 Rest		
1:30 Bell Jump (p64)		2:00 Bell Jump (p64)		2:00 Bell Jump (p64)		
:30 Rest		:30 Rest		:30 Rest		
16 Marching Twists (p104)	Rest	10 Mason Twists (p107)	Rest	10 Cobras (p99)	Rest	Rest
:30 Rest		:30 Rest		:30 Rest		
2:00 Bell Jump (p64)		2:30 Bell Jump (p64)		2:30 Bell Jump (p64)		
:30 Rest		:30 Rest		:30 Rest		
3:00 Basic Jump (p60)		3:30 Basic Jump (p60)		4:30 Basic Jump (p60)		
12 Side Hops (p95)		14 Forward Jumps (p96)		10 Reverse Crunches (p98)		

Prep   WEEK 4

Note: Rest and recovery are vital to the success of the programs and should be included as prescribed on the schedules. Remember also to warm up before your workout and stretch afterward! See pages 84–92 for ideas.

MON	TUE	WED	THU	FRI	SAT	SUN
1:00 Basic Jump (p60)		1:00 Basic Jump (p60)		2:00 Basic Jump (p60)		
:30 Rest		:30 Rest		:30 Rest		
1:00 Skier Jump (p62)		2:00 Bell Jump (p64)		2:00 Skier Jump (p62)		
:30 Rest		:30 Rest		:30 Rest		
2:00 Bell Jump (p64)		2:00 Skier Jump (p62)		2:00 Bell Jump (p64)		
:30 Rest		:30 Rest		:30 Rest		
12 Supermans (p105)	Rest	16 Marching Twists (p104)	Rest	12 Cobras (p99)	Rest	Rest
:30 Rest		:30 Rest		:30 Rest		
2:30 Bell Jump (p64)		2:30 Skier Jump (p62)		2:30 Bell Jump (p64)		
:30 Rest		:30 Rest		:30 Rest		
3:30 Skier Jump (p62)		4:30 Bell Jump (p64)		5:00 Basic Jump (p60)		
12 Hip Raises (p100)		12 Reverse Crunches (p98)		14 Side Hops (p95)		

Basic Program

The Basic Program is the cornerstone of a good jump rope program. We work both easier and intermediate jumps that will tax your overall fitness, muscular endurance and coordination. Be prepared to work and to be challenged. Everyone except for the fittest and most-coordinated jump ropers should go through this program start to finish.

Basic WEEK 1

Note: Rest and recovery are vital to the success of the programs and should be included as prescribed on the schedules. Remember also to warm up before your workout and stretch afterward! See pages 84–92 for ideas.

MON	TUE	WED	THU	FRI	SAT	SUN
10 Supermans (p105)		10 Bird Dogs (p101)		10 Bird Dogs (p101)		
10 Bird Dogs (p101)		10 Hip Raises (p100)		10 Cobras (p99)		
1:00 Basic Jump (p60)		1:00 Basic Jump (p60)		1:00 Basic Jump (p60)		
:30 Rest		:30 Rest		:30 Rest		
1:00 Skier Jump (p62)		1:00 Skier Jump (p62)		2:00 Skier Jump (p62)		
:30 Rest		:30 Rest		:30 Rest		
1:30 Bell Jump (p64)	Rest	2:00 Bell Jump (p64)	Rest	2:00 Bell Jump (p64)	Rest	Rest
:30 Rest		:30 Rest		:30 Rest		
1:30 Skier Jump (p62)		2:00 Skier Jump (p62)		2:00 Skier Jump (p62)		
:30 Rest		:30 Rest		:30 Rest		
2:00 Bell Jump (p64)		2:30 Bell Jump (p64)		2:30 Bell Jump (p64)		
:30 Rest		:30 Rest		:30 Rest		
1:00 Basic Jump (p60)		1:30 Basic Jump (p60)		2:00 Basic Jump (p60)		
20 Marching Twists (p104)		12 Side Hops (p95)		12 Forward Jumps (p96)		

Basic WEEK 2

Note: Rest and recovery are vital to the success of the programs and should be included as prescribed on the schedules. Remember also to warm up before your workout and stretch afterward! See pages 84–92 for ideas.

MON	TUE	WED	THU	FRI	SAT	SUN
10 Cobras (p99)		12 Hip Raises (p100)		12 Cobras (p99)		
10 Supermans (p105)		12 Bird Dogs (p101)		12 Hip Raises (p100)		
1:00 Basic Jump (p60)		1:00 Basic Jump (p60)		2:00 Basic Jump (p60)		
:30 Rest		:30 Rest		:30 Rest		
1:00 Skier Jump (p62)		2:00 Bell Jump (p64)		2:00 Skier Jump (p62)		
:30 Rest		:30 Rest		:30 Rest		
2:00 Bell Jump (p64)	Rest	2:00 Skier Jump (p62)	Rest	2:00 Bell Jump (p64)	Rest	Rest
:30 Rest		:30 Rest		:30 Rest		
2:00 Skier Jump (p62)		2:00 Bell Jump (p64)		2:30 Skier Jump (p62)		
:30 Rest		:30 Rest		:30 Rest		
2:30 Bell Jump (p64)		2:30 Skier Jump (p62)		2:30 Bell Jump (p64)		
:30 Rest		:30 Rest		:30 Rest		
1:30 Skier Jump (p62)		2:00 Bell Jump (p64)		2:30 Basic Jump (p60)		
20 Wood Chops (p99)		16 Side Hops (p95)		16 Forward Jumps (p96)		

Basic   WEEK 3

Note: Rest and recovery are vital to the success of the programs and should be included as prescribed on the schedules. Remember also to warm up before your workout and stretch afterward! See pages 84–92 for ideas.

MON	TUE	WED	THU	FRI	SAT	SUN
12 Hip Raises (p100)		12 Bird Dogs (p101)		14 Hip Raises (p100)		
12 Cobras (p99)		12 Supermans (p105)		14 Bird Dogs (p101)		
1:00 Basic Jump (p60)		1:00 Ali Step Jump (p66)		2:00 Ali Step Jump (p66)		
:30 Rest		:30 Rest		:30 Rest		
1:00 Scissors Jump (p68)		2:00 Scissors Jump (p68)		2:00 Scissors Jump (p68)		
:30 Rest		:30 Rest		:30 Rest		
2:00 Ali Step Jump (p66)	Rest	2:00 Ali Step Jump (p66)	Rest	2:00 Alt Single-Leg Jump (p70)	Rest	Rest
:30 Rest		:30 Rest		:30 Rest		
2:00 Skier Jump (p62)		2:00 Alt Single-Leg Jump (p70)		2:30 Ali Step Jump (p66)		
:30 Rest		:30 Rest		:30 Rest		
2:30 Bell Jump (p64)		2:30 Skier Jump (p62)		2:30 Scissors Jump (p68)		
:30 Rest		:30 Rest		:30 Rest		
2:30 Skier Jump (p62)		3:00 Bell Jump (p64)		3:00 Basic Jump (p60)		
16 Bicycle Crunches (p109)		22 Wood Chops (p99)		20 Forward Jumps (p96)		

Basic   WEEK 4

Note: Rest and recovery are vital to the success of the programs and should be included as prescribed on the schedules. Remember also to warm up before your workout and stretch afterward! See pages 84–92 for ideas.

MON	TUE	WED	THU	FRI	SAT	SUN
14 Hip Raises (p100)		16 Bird Dogs (p101)		16 Hip Raises (p100)		
14 Bird Dogs (p101)		16 Supermans (p105)		16 Cobras (p99)		
3:00 Ali Step Jump (p66)		3:00 Ali Step Jump (p66)		3:00 Ali Step Jump (p66)		
:30 Rest		:30 Rest		:30 Rest		
2:30 Scissors Jump (p68)		3:00 Scissors Jump (p68)		3:00 Scissors Jump (p68)		
:30 Rest		:30 Rest		:30 Rest		
2:30 Alt Single-Leg Jump (p70)	Rest	3:00 Alt Single-Leg Jump (p70)	Rest	3:00 Alt Single-Leg Jump (p70)	Rest	Rest
:30 Rest		:30 Rest		:30 Rest		
:30 Single-Leg Hop (left) (p74)		:45 Single-Leg Hop (left) (p74)		2:30 Scissors Jump (p68)		
:30 Rest		:30 Rest		:30 Rest		
:30 Single-Leg Hop (right) (p74)		:45 Single-Leg Hop (right) (p74)		2:30 Scissors Jump (p68)		
:30 Rest		:30 Rest		:30 Rest		
6:00 Basic Jump (p60)		6:00 Basic Jump (p60)		6:00 Basic Jump (p60)		
22 Side Hops (p95)		20 Bicycle Crunches (p109)		22 Wood Chops (p99)		

Advanced Program

The Advanced Program is seven weeks of grueling work, extreme jumps and an all-out blitz on your ability to jump and recover. This program will have you sucking wind, burning muscles and sweating like you've never sweat before. Those that stick with this for the full seven weeks will be in better shape than they could ever believe from "just jumping rope." We promise that when you complete this program you'll never ever say "just jumping rope" again!

Advanced   WEEK 1

Note: Rest and recovery are vital to the success of the programs and should be included as prescribed on the schedules. Remember also to warm up before your workout and stretch afterward! See pages 84–92 for ideas.

MON	TUE	WED	THU	FRI	SAT	SUN
22 Supermans (p105)		20 Hip Raises (p100)		22 Cobras (p99)		
20 Marching Twists (p104)		20 Side Hops (p95)		22 Side Hops (p95)		
1:00 Basic Jump (p60)		1:00 Ali Step Jump (p66)		1:00 Ali Step Jump (p66)		
:30 Rest		:30 Rest		:30 Rest		
1:00 Scissors Jump (p68)		2:00 Scissors Jump (p68)		2:00 Scissors Jump (p68)		
2:00 Ali Step Jump (p66)		2:00 Ali Step Jump (p66)		2:00 Alt Single-Leg Jump (p70)		
:30 Rest	Rest	:30 Rest	Rest	:30 Rest	Rest	Rest
2:00 Skier Jump (p62)		2:00 Alt Single-Leg Jump (p70)		2:30 Ali Step Jump (p66)		
:30 Rest		:30 Rest		:30 Rest		
22 Wood Chops (p99)		24 Marching Twists (p104)		22 Forward Jumps (p96)		
1:00 Bell Jump (p64)		1:30 Skier Jump (p62)		1:30 Scissors Jump (p68)		
:30 Rest		:30 Rest		:30 Rest		
2:30 Skier Jump (p62)		2:30 Bell Jump (p64)		2:30 Basic Jump (p60)		
16 Leg Lifts (p102)		18 Reverse Crunches (p98)		18 Mason Twists (p107)		

Advanced WEEK 2

Note: Rest and recovery are vital to the success of the programs and should be included as prescribed on the schedules. Remember also to warm up before your workout and stretch afterward! See pages 84–92 for ideas.

MON	TUE	WED	THU	FRI	SAT	SUN
22 Hip Raises (p100)		22 Cobras (p99)		20 Supermans (p105)		
22 Forward Jumps (p96)		24 Side Hops (p95)		26 Marching Twists (p104)		
1:30 Ali Step Jump (p66)		1:30 Ali Step Jump (p66)		1:30 Ali Step Jump (p66)		
:30 Rest		:30 Rest		:30 Rest		
2:30 Scissors Jump (p68)		3:00 Scissors Jump (p68)		3:00 Scissors Jump (p68)		
:30 Rest		:30 Rest		:30 Rest		
10 Squat Jumps (p97)		28 Marching Twists (p104)		22 Mountain Climbers (p106)		
1:30 Alt Single-Leg Jump (p70)	Rest	1:00 Alt Single-Leg Jump (p70)	Rest	1:00 Alt Single-Leg Jump (p70)	Rest	Rest
:30 Rest		:30 Rest		:30 Rest		
1:00 Single-Leg Hop (left) (p74)		1:30 Single-Leg Hop (left) (p74)		2:30 Single Leg (left) (p74)		
:30 Rest		:30 Rest		:30 Rest		
1:00 Single-Leg Hop (right) (p74)		1:30 Single-Leg Hop (right) (p74)		2:30 Single Leg (right) (p74)		
:30 Rest		:30 Rest		:30 Rest		
3:00 Basic Jump (p60)		3:00 Basic Jump (p60)		3:30 Basic Jump (p60)		
20 Bicycle Crunches (p109)		22 Leg Lifts (p102)		24 Reverse Crunches (p98)		

Advanced   WEEK 3

Note: Rest and recovery are vital to the success of the programs and should be included as prescribed on the schedules. Remember also to warm up before your workout and stretch afterward! See pages 84–92 for ideas.

MON	TUE	WED	THU	FRI	SAT	SUN
22 Cobras (p99)		24 Hip Raises (p100)		22 Supermans (p105)		
24 Mountain Climbers (p106)		22 Wood Chops (p99)		20 Forward Jumps (p96)		
1:30 Ali Step Jump (p66)		1:30 Ali Step Jump (p66)		1:30 Ali Step Jump (p66)		
:30 Rest		:30 Rest		:30 Rest		
3:00 Scissors Jump (p68)		3:00 Scissors Jump (p68)		1:00 Double Under (p72)		
:30 Rest		:30 Rest		:30 Rest		
:30 Double Under (p72)	Rest	:45 Double Under (p72)	Rest	1:00 Double Under (p72)	Rest	Rest
:30 Rest		1:00 Rest		1:00 Rest		
:30 Double Under (p72)		:45 Double Under (p72)		1:00 Double Under (p72)		
:30 Rest		1:00 Rest		1:00 Rest		
:30 Double Under (p72)		1:00 Double Under (p72)		:30 Running Man (p76)		
:30 Rest		1:30 Rest		1:30 Rest		
3:30 Basic Jump (p60)		3:30 Basic Jump (p60)		3:00 Basic Jump (p60)		
22 Bicycle Crunches (p109)		24 Mason Twists (p107)		24 Leg Lifts (p102)		

Advanced   WEEK 4

Note: Rest and recovery are vital to the success of the programs and should be included as prescribed on the schedules. Remember also to warm up before your workout and stretch afterward! See pages 84–92 for ideas.

MON	TUE	WED	THU	FRI	SAT	SUN
24 Hip Raises (p100)		22 Cobras (p99)		24 Bird Dogs (p101)		
22 Forward Jumps (p96)		24 Side Hops (p95)		24 Mountain Climbers (p106)		
1:30 Alt Single-Leg Jump (p70)		1:30 Alt Single-Leg Jump (p70)		1:30 Ali Step Jump (p66)		
:30 Rest		:30 Rest		:30 Rest		
24 Mountain Climbers (p106)		8 Inchworms (p108)		12 Squat Jumps (p97)		
1:30 Alt Single-Leg Jump (p70)	Rest	1:30 Alt Single-Leg Jump (p70)	Rest	1:30 Scissors Jump (p68)	Rest	Rest
1:00 Rest		1:00 Rest		:30 Rest		
:30 Single-Leg Hop (left) (p74)		1:00 Single-Leg Hop (left) (p74)		3:00 Alt Single-Leg Jump (p70)		
1:00 Rest		1:00 Rest		:30 Rest		
:30 Single-Leg Hop (right) (p74)		1:00 Single-Leg Hop (right) (p74)		1:30 Scissors Jump (p68)		
1:00 Rest		1:00 Rest		:30 Rest		
1:00 Double Under (p72)		1:00 Running Man (p76)		2:30 Skier Jump (p62)		
1:30 Rest		1:30 Rest		:30 Rest		
4:00 Basic Jump (p60)		4:00 Basic Jump (p60)		4:00 Basic Jump (p60)		
26 Leg Lifts (p102)		24 Reverse Crunches (p98)		26 Bicycle Crunches (p109)		

Advanced   WEEK 5

Note: Rest and recovery are vital to the success of the programs and should be included as prescribed on the schedules. Remember also to warm up before your workout and stretch afterward! See pages 84–92 for ideas.

MON	TUE	WED	THU	FRI	SAT	SUN
22 Bird Dogs (p101)		24 Hip Raises (p100)		24 Supermans (p105)		
22 Mason Twists (p107)		26 Reverse Crunches (p98)		26 Leg Lifts (p102)		
2:00 Alt Single-Leg Jump (p70)		2:00 Alt Single-Leg Jump (p70)		2:00 Alt Single-Leg Jump (p70)		
1:00 Rest		1:00 Rest		1:00 Rest		
10 Squat Jumps (p97)		12 Squat Jumps (p97)		10 Inchworms (p108)		
2:00 Alt Single-Leg Jump (p70)		2:00 Running Man (p76)		2:00 Running Man (p76)		
1:00 Rest		1:00 Rest		1:00 Rest		
1:00 Single-Leg Hop (left) (p74)	Rest	1:00 Double Under (p72)	Rest	1:00 Double Under (p72)	Rest	Rest
1:00 Rest		1:00 Rest		:30 Rest		
1:00 Single-Leg Hop (right) (p74)		1:00 Double Under (p72)		1:00 Double Under (p72)		
1:00 Rest		1:00 Rest		:30 Rest		
1:00 Double Under (p72)		2:00 Running Man (p76)		2:00 Running Man (p76)		
1:30 Rest		1:30 Rest		:30 Rest		
4:30 Basic Jump (p60)		4:30 Basic Jump (p60)		5:00 Basic Jump (p60)		
26 Reverse Crunches (p98)		26 Bicycle Crunches (p109)		28 Mason Twists (p107)		

Advanced WEEK 6

Note: Rest and recovery are vital to the success of the programs and should be included as prescribed on the schedules. Remember also to warm up before your workout and stretch afterward! See pages 84–92 for ideas.

MON	TUE	WED	THU	FRI	SAT	SUN
22 Cobras (p99)		24 Supermans (p105)		24 Bird Dogs (p101)		
22 Leg Lifts (p102)		30 Reverse Crunches (p98)		26 Mason Twists (p107)		
1:00 Running Man (p76)		1:00 Running Man (p76)		1:00 Running Man (p76)		
:30 Rest		:30 Rest		:30 Rest		
1:30 Single-Leg Hop (left) (p74)		1:30 Single-Leg Hop (left) (p74)		1:00 Knee Tuck Single (p78)		
1:00 Rest		1:00 Rest		1:00 Rest		
1:30 Single-Leg Hop (right) (p74)		1:30 Single-Leg Hop (right) (p74)		2:00 Double Under (p72)		
1:00 Rest	Rest	1:00 Rest	Rest	1:00 Rest	Rest	Rest
3:00 Running Man (p76)		1:00 Knee Tuck Single (p78)		1:00 Knee Tuck Double (p80)		
1:00 Rest		1:00 Rest		1:00 Rest		
1:00 Knee Tuck Single (p78)		:30 Knee Tuck Double (p80)		2:00 Double Under (p72)		
10 Squat Jumps (p97)		10 Inchworms (p108)		12 Squat Jumps (p97)		
22 Marching Twists (p104)		20 Wood Chops (p99)		18 Forward Jumps (p96)		
1:00 Rest		1:00 Rest		1:00 Rest		
5:00 Basic Jump (p60)		5:00 Basic Jump (p60)		5:00 Basic Jump (p60)		

Advanced WEEK 7

Note: Rest and recovery are vital to the success of the programs and should be included as prescribed on the schedules. Remember also to warm up before your workout and stretch afterward! See pages 84–92 for ideas.

MON	TUE	WED	THU	FRI	SAT	SUN
24 Supermans (p105)		24 Hip Raises (p100)		24 Bird Dogs (p101)		
3:00 Running Man (p76)		2:00 Double Under (p72)		2:00 Double Under (p72)		
2:00 Knee Tuck Single (p78)		2:00 Knee Tuck Single (p78)		2:00 Knee Tuck Double (p80)		
:30 Rest		:30 Rest		:30 Rest		
2:00 Double Under (p72)		2:00 Double Under (p72)		2:00 Double Under (p72)		
12 Inchworms (p108)		12 Squat Jumps (p97)		12 Squat Jumps (p97)		
1:00 Rest	Rest	1:00 Rest	Rest	1:00 Rest	Rest	Rest
2:00 Knee Tuck Double (p80)		2:00 Knee Tuck Double (p80)		2:00 Knee Tuck Double (p80)		
1:00 Rest		1:00 Rest		1:00 Rest		
2:00 Double Under (p72)		2:00 Double Under (p72)		2:00 Double Under (p72)		
4:00 Basic Jump (p60)		4:00 Basic Jump (p60)		4:00 Basic Jump (p60)		
:30 Rest		:30 Rest		:30 Rest		
26 Bicycle Crunches (p109)		30 Mason Twists (p107)		30 Leg Lifts (p102)		

Next Steps

Congratulations! If you've gotten through the entire program, there's a good chance you've just accomplished the most physically demanding achievement in your life. Take a moment to let that sink in and realize you're capable of much more than you may have previously dreamed possible.

Now, take a deep breath and absorb the next statement: This is only the beginning of a New You. You have the opportunity to write the next chapter of your fitness and athletic ability.

What challenge comes after jumping rope? Well, anything does! Now's the time to set your goals, challenge yourself and make your fitness dreams a reality. If you want to run a marathon, train for a triathlon, gain muscle, lose weight, get ripped, get stronger or generally feel better about yourself, we've written additional books and created many challenges that'll help you set and achieve new goals—and transform your life in the process. Each new challenge will make you dig deep like this program did to make you stronger, fitter and healthier than you'd ever thought possible. Check out all our books and review the free online programs at www.7weekstofitness.com. Make a choice and set your sights on a New You.

PART 3:
THE JUMPS

"Jumping rope" doesn't need to be the same jump over and over again. We describe and illustrate a number of variations to the single jump in this book. Each jump has its own distinct benefits and targets specific training. Football or soccer players can benefit from the Alternating Single-Leg jump (page 70) while marathoners can perform Scissors (page 68)

to build leg and hip strength to carry them through the long miles. It bears to mention that you don't need to be an alpine enthusiast to enjoy The Skier (page 62)—each technique was created to benefit individuals of all athletic ability.

All jumps will use the classic grip (see page 33).

Shadow Jumping

DIFFICULTY ★☆☆☆☆   INTENSITY ★☆☆☆☆

Shadow jumping is the ultimate in easy jumping. There's no rope to trip you up, no need for coordination, no timing of jumping the rope and no worry about hand position. Just start jumping. That means there's never an excuse for not jumping, either.

1 Stand erect with your feet approximately shoulder-width apart, knees slightly bent and arms extended along your sides. Throughout the movement your weight should be distributed evenly on the balls of both feet. Pretend to grab the handles of a jump rope and hold them at your sides. You'll use a pretend jump rope throughout the exercise.

TIP: Maintain your balance, focus on being "light on your feet" and try to find your rhythm. The shadow jump is the perfect way to get good at jumping rope without worrying about the rope.

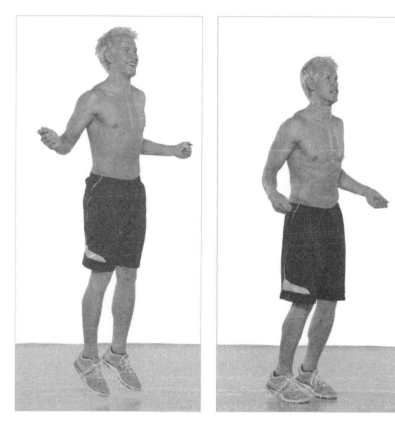

2 Pretend to swing the rope overheard and forward. It might seem strange to swing an imaginary jump rope, but it'll help when you move to more advanced jumps. Jump with both feet as the imaginary jump rope passes beneath them.

3 Land on the balls of both feet and bend your knees slightly to cushion the impact while continuing to rotate your wrists and swing the pretend rope in an arc from back to front.

Basic Jump

DIFFICULTY ★★☆☆☆   INTENSITY ★★☆☆☆

This is the jump that immediately comes to mind when someone says "jumping rope." Everyone should start with this move since nearly every advanced jump in this program is based on the easiest-to-master jump. Once you learn the proper technique and get your rhythm down, this is the (excuse the pun) jumping-off point to move up to the more advanced jumps. Just because it's "basic" doesn't mean it's inferior by any means— this jump will work your legs, glutes and core and also tax your cardiovascular system to burn calories and fat efficiently and effectively.

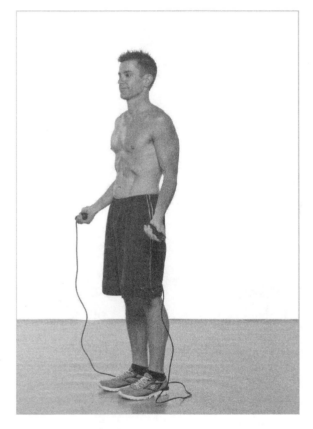

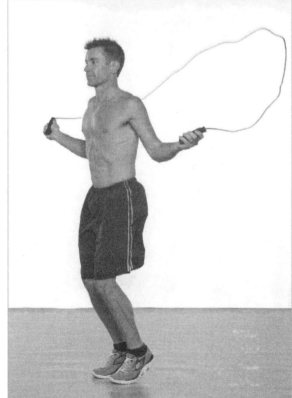

1 Stand erect with your feet approximately shoulder-width apart, knees slightly bent and arms extended along your sides. Throughout the movement your weight should be distributed evenly on the balls of both feet. Grip the jump rope handles using a classic grip. Extend the apex of the jump rope loop on the ground behind your feet.

2 Rotate your wrists forward to swing the rope overhead. The first movement from a dead stop will require more arm and shoulder movement, but as you progress on subsequent jumps, your arms should remain in a semi-static downward position along the sides of your body and your hands should rotate in small arcs.

TIP: Maintain your balance and time your jumps based on the speed of the rope. As you progress, focus on being "light on your feet" by jumping and landing in a controlled manner. Breathe slowly and rhythmically—make sure you don't hold your breath!

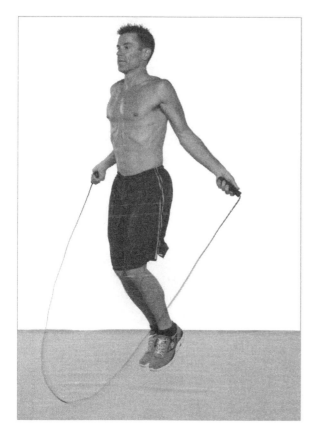

3 As the apex of the rope's loop approaches the ground in front of your body and is 6 inches away from your toes, jump straight up approximately 4 to 6 inches off the floor with both feet as the rope passes underneath.

4 Land on the balls of both feet and bend your knees slightly to cushion the impact while continuing to rotate your wrists and swing the rope in an arc from back to front.

The Skier

DIFFICULTY ★★☆☆☆   INTENSITY ★★☆☆☆

This side-to-side jump is great for developing lateral strength, which all athletes need.

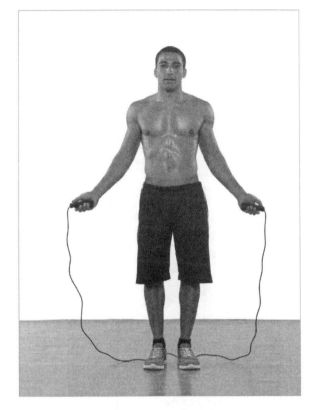

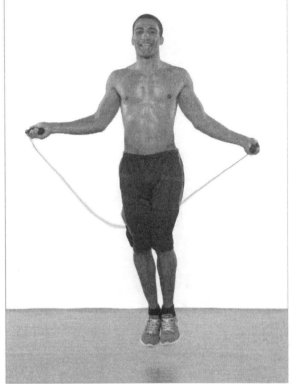

1 Stand erect with your feet approximately shoulder-width apart, knees slightly bent and arms extended along your sides. Throughout the movement your weight should be distributed evenly on the balls of both feet. Grip the jump rope handles using a classic grip. Extend the apex of the jump rope loop on the ground behind your feet.

2–3 Rotate your wrists forward to swing the rope overhead. Your arms should remain in a semi-static downward position along the sides of your body and your hands should rotate in small arcs. As the apex of the rope's loop approaches the ground in front of your body and is 6 inches away from your toes, jump laterally to the side with

both feet, approximately 2 to 6 inches (farther is harder) from your starting point, as the rope passes underneath. Land on the balls of both feet and bend your knees slightly to cushion the impact while continuing to rotate your wrists and swing the rope in an arc from back to front.

4 As the apex of the rope's loop approaches the ground in front of your body and is 6 inches away from your toes, jump laterally to the opposite side approximately 2 to 6 inches (farther is harder), returning to your starting point as the rope passes underneath. Your upper body remains relatively static, not moving too much. Your feet do most of the traveling and lead the way.

The Bell

DIFFICULTY ★★☆☆☆   INTENSITY ★★☆☆☆

This jump is much like The Skier, except you jump forward and backward. The Bell develops good ankle proprioception and hip strength.

1 Stand erect with your feet approximately shoulder-width apart, knees slightly bent and arms extended along your sides. Throughout the movement your weight should be distributed evenly on the balls of both feet. Grip the jump rope handles using a classic grip. Extend the apex of the jump rope loop on the ground behind your feet.

2–3 Rotate your wrists forward to swing the rope overhead. Your arms should remain in a semi-static downward position along the sides of your body and your hands should rotate in small arcs. As the apex of the rope's loop approaches the ground in front of your body and is 6 inches away from your toes, jump forward approximately 2 to 6

TIP: Start small. The longer your jump, the harder the exercise. As you find your rhythm, you'll get into a flow and find you're jumping back and forth with ease.

inches (farther is harder) from your starting point with both feet as the rope passes underneath. Land on the balls of both feet and bend your knees slightly to cushion the impact while continuing to rotate your wrists and swing the rope in an arc from back to front.

4 As the apex of the rope's loop approaches the ground in front of your body and is 6 inches away from your toes, jump backward approximately 2 to 6 inches (farther is harder), returning to your starting point as the rope passes underneath. Your upper body remains relatively static, not moving too much. Your feet do most of the traveling and lead the way.

Ali Step

DIFFICULTY ★★★★☆   INTENSITY ★★★☆☆

This iconic heel-to-toe jump was made famous by boxer Muhammad Ali. The Ali Step develops coordination and is a great way to blast through calories without being too tough on the body.

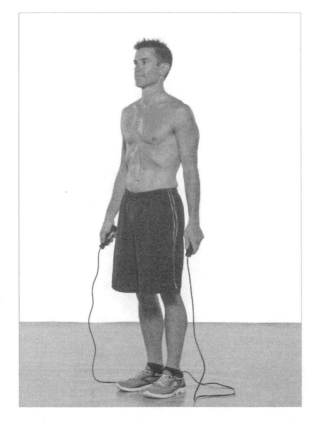

1 Stand erect with your feet approximately shoulder-width apart, knees slightly bent and arms extended along your sides. Throughout the movement your weight should be distributed evenly on the balls of both feet. Grip the jump rope handles using a classic grip. Extend the apex of the jump rope loop on the ground behind your feet.

2 – 3 Rotate your wrists forward to swing the rope overhead. Your arms should remain in a semi-static downward position along the sides of your body and your hands should rotate in small arcs. As the apex of the rope's loop approaches the ground in front of your body and is 6 inches away from your toes, hop on your right foot and touch your

TIP: Don't get frustrated. This jump takes coordination. Give it time and you'll end up loving this jump as a steady-state workout that avoids boredom!

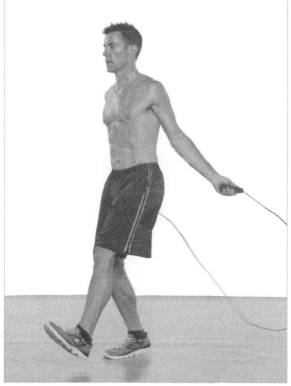

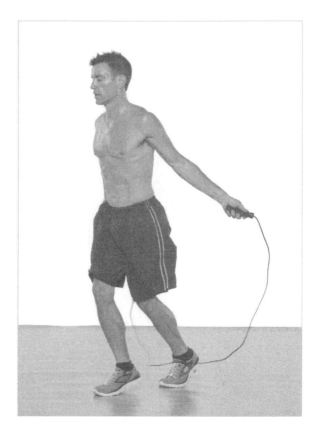

left heel lightly to the ground just in front of you. Land on the ball of your right foot and bend your knee slightly to cushion the impact while continuing to rotate your wrists and swing the rope in an arc from back to front.

4 As the apex of the rope's loop approaches the ground in front of your body and is 6 inches away from your toe, hop on your right foot and touch your left toe lightly to the ground just behind you.

Repeat steps 1 through 4 on the opposite side.

Scissors

DIFFICULTY ★★★☆☆   INTENSITY ★★★★☆

A great all-around burner, this split jump ranks up there in intensity and should be a staple of any jump rope program. You can alter the intensity by stepping your feet apart farther.

1 Stand erect with your feet approximately shoulder-width apart, knees slightly bent and arms extended along your sides. Throughout the movement your weight should be distributed evenly on the balls of both feet. Grip the jump rope handles using a classic grip. Extend the apex of the jump rope loop on the ground behind your feet.

2 Rotate your wrists forward to swing the rope overhead. Your arms should remain in a semi-static downward position along the sides of your body and your hands should rotate in small arcs. As the apex of the rope's loop approaches the ground in front of your body and is 6 inches away from your toes, jump your right foot forward approximately 2 inches and simultaneously jump your left foot backward 2 inches. Your legs should be split (hence the name "Scissors"). Land on the balls of both feet and bend your knees slightly to cushion the impact while continuing to rotate your wrists and swing the rope in an arc from back to front.

TIP: Start small. The longer the separation between your feet, the harder the exercise.

3 As the apex of the rope's loop approaches the ground in front of your body and is 6 inches away from your toes, jump your right foot backward approximately 4 inches (moving past your starting point) and simultaneously jump your left foot forward 4 inches. Your feet have now traded places in one jump. The Scissor never returns to the starting position until you're done. Your feet travel past neutral on each jump, trading places on each swing of the rope.

Alternating Single Leg

DIFFICULTY ★★☆☆☆   INTENSITY ★★★★☆

This jump will tax each leg individually in alternating fashion and develop both coordination and leg strength. If someone were to look at you from the side, it'd roughly look like you were running in place. Be forewarned: This jump will get your heart pumping!

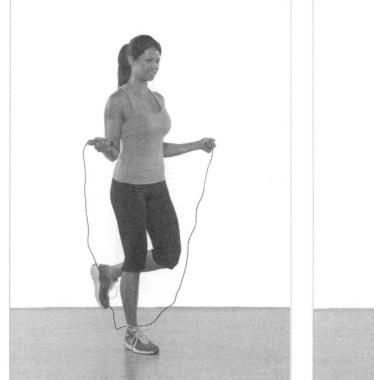

1 Stand erect with your feet approximately shoulder-width apart, knees slightly bent and arms extended along your sides. Shift your weight completely to your right foot and lift your left foot off the ground approximately 6 inches. Throughout the movement your weight should be distributed unevenly on the ball of one foot. One foot should support 100% of your weight while the other leg is tucked under your body in a runner's pose. Grip the jump rope handles using a classic grip. Extend the apex of the jump rope loop on the ground behind your feet.

2 – 3 Rotate your wrists forward to swing the rope overhead. Your arms should remain in a semi-static downward position along the sides of your body and your hands should rotate in small arcs. As the apex of the rope's loop approaches the ground in front of your body and is 6 inches away from your toes, jump off your right foot and

TIP: Go easy. You're beginning to stress one leg more than the other and patience is a virtue in this case. Build up to long jumps. Let your body adapt.

simultaneously bring your left foot to the ground. Tuck your right foot under your body in a runner's pose. Land on the ball of your left foot and bend your knee slightly to cushion the impact while continuing to rotate your wrists and swing the rope in an arc from back to front.

4 As the apex of the rope's loop approaches the ground in front of your body and is 6 inches away from your toes, jump off your left foot and simultaneously bring your right foot to the ground, returning to starting position.

Double Under

DIFFICULTY ★★★★☆   INTENSITY ★★★★★

This is the Basic Jump (page 60) on steroids. The rope travels underneath your body twice per jump. That's right, twice. Give this jump 20 jumps and you'll have sweat pouring out of places you never knew you had!

1 Stand erect with your feet approximately shoulder-width apart, knees slightly bent and arms extended along your sides. Throughout the movement your weight should be distributed evenly on the balls of both feet. Grip the jump rope handles using a classic grip. Extend the apex of the jump rope loop on the ground behind your feet.

2 Rotate your wrists forward to swing the rope overhead. Your arms should remain in a semi-static downward position along the sides of your body and your hands should rotate in small arcs. As the apex of the rope's loop approaches the ground in front of your body and is 6 inches away from your toes, jump straight up approximately 6 to 8 inches off the floor with both feet as the rope passes underneath.

TIP: Start with the Basic Jump. Once you gain momentum, increase your swing speed and attempt a Double Under. Alternate between Basic Jump and Double Under until you're able to perform multiple doubles back to back.

3 Continue your swing quickly while your feet are still off the ground and complete another swing under your feet.

4 Land on the balls of both feet and bend your knees slightly to cushion the impact while continuing to rotate your wrists and swing the rope in an arc from back to front.

Single-Leg Hop

DIFFICULTY ★★★☆☆   INTENSITY ★★★★☆

Simply hop on one leg as you jump. Think of it this way: You're using half your legs (aka, base and strength) for the Basic Jump, so the hop should be twice as hard. Get ready to work!

1 Stand erect with your feet approximately shoulder-width apart, knees slightly bent and arms extended along your sides. Shift your weight completely to your right foot and lift your left foot off the ground approximately 6 inches. Throughout the movement your weight should be distributed unevenly on the ball of one foot. One foot should support 100% of your weight while the other leg is tucked under your body in a runner's pose. Grip the jump rope handles using a classic grip. Extend the apex of the jump rope loop on the ground behind your feet.

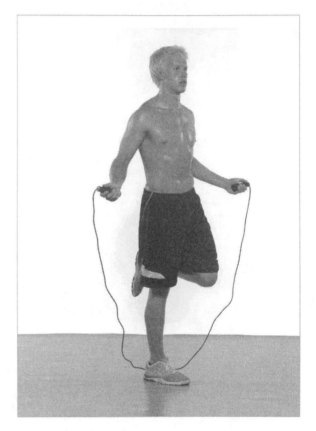

TIP: When switching from your right leg to your left leg, you can either perform a single-leg hop and keep going on your left or completely stop your jump and restart with your left leg as the primary. This is a personal preference.

TIP: Go easy. Single-Leg Hop really taxes your legs and you'll need to develop some serious strength in your legs to complete long jump sequences. Be patient and let your body adapt.

2 – 3 Rotate your wrists forward to swing the rope overhead. Your arms should remain in a semi-static downward position along the sides of your body and your hands should rotate in small arcs. As the apex of the rope's loop approaches the ground in front of your body and is 6 inches away from your toes, jump off your right foot. Keep your left foot tucked under your body. Land on the ball of your right foot and bend your knee slightly to cushion the impact while continuing to rotate your wrists and swing the rope in an arc from back to front.

Once you've done the prescribed number of reps on your right leg, switch to jumping with your left.

Running Man

DIFFICULTY ★★★★☆   INTENSITY ★★★★★

Want more running in your jump rope? Like the idea of mixing wind sprints with jumping rope? This high-knee jump is for you! Run in place while jumping. I guarantee you'll feel like you've just finished an hour of wind sprints when you're done with these.

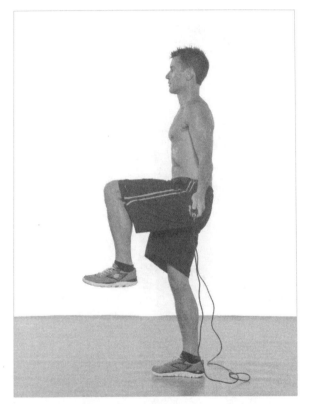

1 Stand erect with your feet approximately shoulder-width apart, knees slightly bent and arms extended along your sides. Shift your weight completely to your right foot and lift your left knee to about hip height (this will differ for everyone depending on flexibility). Throughout the movement your weight should be distributed unevenly on the ball of one foot. One foot should support 100% of your weight while the other leg comes in front of your body. Grip the jump rope handles using a classic grip. Extend the apex of the jump rope loop on the ground behind your feet.

2 – 3 Rotate your wrists forward to swing the rope overhead. Your arms should remain in a semi-static downward position along the sides of your body and your hands should rotate in small arcs. As the apex of the rope's loop approaches the ground in front of your body and is 6 inches away from your toes, jump off your right foot and simultaneously bring your left foot to the ground. Lift your right knee to about hip height. Land on the ball of your left foot and bend your knee slightly to cushion the impact while continuing to rotate your wrists and swing the rope in an arc from back to front.

TIP: Go easy. You're beginning to stress one leg more than the other and patience is a virtue in this case. Build up to long jumps. Let your body adapt.

4 As the apex of the rope's loop approaches the ground in front of your body and is 6 inches away from your toes, jump off your left foot and simultaneously bring your right foot to the ground, returning to starting position.

Knee Tuck Single

DIFFICULTY ★★★★☆   INTENSITY ★★★★★

This and Double Tuck are the hardest jumps to sequence in both rhythm and stamina. Work your way into the tucks. This relatively "slow" jump delivers where it counts. Jump, tuck your knees and continue until you can't jump anymore. That should be pretty quick.

1 Stand erect with your feet approximately shoulder-width apart, knees slightly bent and arms extended along your sides. Throughout the movement your weight should be distributed evenly on the balls of both feet. Grip the jump rope handles using a classic grip. Extend the apex of the jump rope loop on the ground behind your feet.

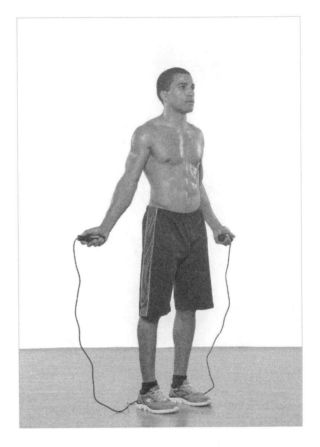

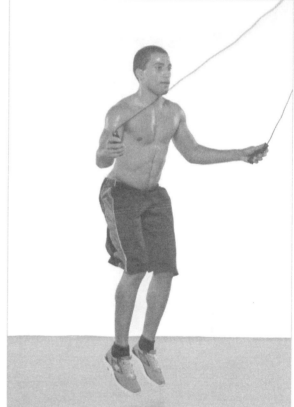

2 – 3 Rotate your wrists forward to swing the rope overhead. Your arms should remain in a semi-static downward position along the sides of your body and your hands should rotate in small arcs. As the apex of the rope's loop approaches the ground in front of your body and is 6 inches away from your toes, jump straight up and bring your knees toward your chest, hip level or higher. Land on the balls of both feet and bend your knees slightly to cushion the impact while continuing to rotate your wrists and swing the rope in an arc from back to front.

That's one jump. Continue in rhythm to sequence.

Knee Tuck Double

DIFFICULTY ★★★★★   INTENSITY ★★★★★

The Double Tuck is one of the hardest jumps to sequence in both rhythm and stamina. Work your way up to it. It doesn't get harder than this. Jump, tuck, swing the rope beneath you twice. You have to jump and tuck your knees high enough and swing the rope fast enough for it to go around twice before you land and do it all over again. DO NOT TAKE THIS JUMP LIGHTLY!

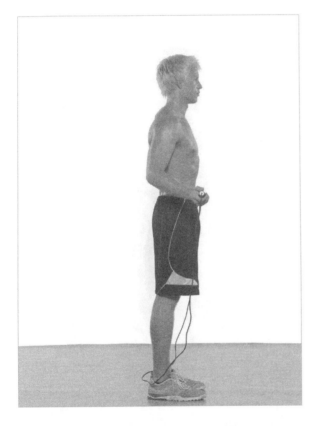

1 Stand erect with your feet approximately shoulder-width apart, knees slightly bent and arms extended along your sides. Throughout the movement your weight should be distributed evenly on the balls of both feet. Grip the jump rope handles using a classic grip. Extend the apex of the jump rope loop on the ground behind your feet.

2 Rotate your wrists forward to swing the rope overhead. Your arms should remain in a semi-static downward position along the sides of your body and your hands should rotate in small arcs. As the apex of the rope's loop approaches the ground in front of your body and is 6 inches away from your toes, jump straight up and bring your knees toward your chest, hip level or higher.

TIP: Adequate swing speed and a high jump are required to perform a Double Tuck. Start with a Basic Jump and build up your momentum, explode off the ground from the balls of your feet and accelerate your swing speed to attempt a Double Tuck. Alternate between Basic Jump and Double Tuck until you can perform doubles back to back.

3 Continue your swing quickly while your feet are still off the ground and complete another swing under your feet.

4 Land on the balls of both feet and bend your knees slightly to cushion the impact while continuing to rotate your wrists and swing the rope in an arc from back to front.

That's one jump. Continue in rhythm to sequence.

APPENDIX

Warming Up

Properly warming up the body prior to any activity is very important, as is stretching post-workout (see page 89). Please note that warming up and stretching are two completely different things: A warm-up routine should be done before stretching so that your muscles are more pliable and able to be stretched efficiently. You should not "warm up" by stretching; you simply don't want to push, pull or stretch cold muscles.

Prior to warm-up, your muscles are significantly less flexible. Think of pulling a rubber band out of a freezer: If you stretch it forcefully before it has a chance to warm up, you'll likely tear it. Stretching cold muscles can cause a significantly higher rate of muscle strains and even injuries to joints that rely on those muscles for alignment.

It's crucial to raise your body temperature prior to beginning a workout. In order to prevent injury, such as a muscle strain, you want to loosen up your muscles and joints before you begin the actual exercise movement. A good warm-up before your workout should slowly raise your core body temperature, heart rate and breathing. Before jumping into the workout, you must increase blood flow to all working areas of the body. This augmented blood flow will transport more oxygen and nutrients to the muscles being worked. The warm-up will also increase the range of motion of your joints.

Another goal is to focus your mental awareness and body proprioception. You've heard that meditation requires being present in the "Now." The same is true for a demanding exercise routine. Being totally present and focused will help you perform better and avoid injury.

A warm-up should consist of light physical activity (such as walking, jogging in place, stationary biking, jumping jacks, etc.) and only take between 5–10 minutes to complete. Your individual fitness level and the activity determine how hard and how long you should go but, generally speaking, the average person should build up to a light sweat during warm-up. You want to prepare your body for activity, not fatigue it.

A warm-up should be done in these stages:

GENTLE MOBILITY   Easy movements that get your joints moving freely, like arm and shoulder circles and neck rotations.

PULSE RAISING   Gentle, progressive, aerobic activity that starts the process of raising your heart rate, like jumping jacks.

SPECIFIC MOBILITY   This begins working the joints and muscles that will be used during the activity. Perform the following dynamic movements to prepare your body for the upcoming jump rope workout. Dynamic movements should raise the heart rate, loosen specific joints and muscles, and get you motivated for your workout.

Ankle Circles

If you need help with balance, you can use a wall, desk or chair.

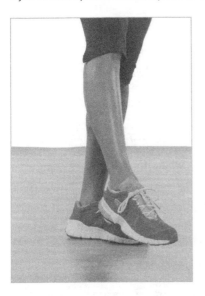

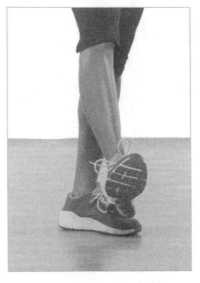

1 Stand with your feet shoulder-width apart. Raise your left foot approximately 2 inches and perform a clockwise rotation with your big toe. Repeat 10–20 times.

2 Perform a counter-clockwise rotation with your big toe. Repeat 10–20 times.

Switch sides.

Wrist Circles

1 Stand with your feet shoulder-width apart and your arms extended horizontally in front of your body. Rotate both hands outward at the same time. Repeat 10–20 times.

2 Rotate both hands inward at the same time. Repeat 10–20 times.

Hip Circles

1 Stand with your feet shoulder-width apart. Engage your core, making sure you have some tension in your upper and lower abdominals as well as lower back. Slowly circle your hips to the right. Make a full revolution, returning back to starting position. Repeat 10–20 times.

2 Slowly circle your hips to the left. Make a full revolution, returning back to starting position. Repeat 10–20 times.

Arm Circles

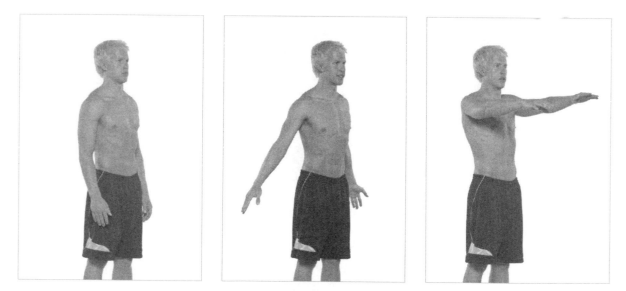

1 Stand with your feet shoulder-width apart.

2 – 3 Move both arms in a complete circle forward 5 times and then backward 5 times.

Jumping Jacks

1 Stand tall with your feet slightly less than shoulder width apart and arms extended along your sides, palms facing forward.

2 Jump 6–12 inches off the ground and simultaneously spread your feet apart an additional 20–30 inches while extending your hands directly overhead.

Jump 6–12 inches off the ground and return your hands and feet to the starting position. Do 10 reps.

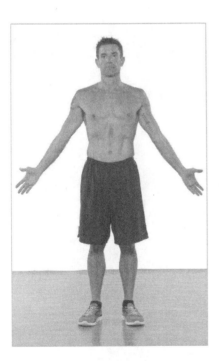

Stretching

Stretching should generally be done after a workout. It'll help you reduce soreness from the workout, increase range of motion and flexibility within a joint or muscle and prepare your body for any future workouts. Stretching immediately post-exercise while your muscles are still warm allows your muscles to return to their full range of motion (which gives you more flexibility gains) and reduces the chance of injury or fatigue in the hours or days after an intense workout. It's important to remember that even when you're warm and loose, you should never "bounce" during stretching. Keep your movements slow and controlled.

Required Stretches

There are two specific stretches you should do after each workout: the wall push-up and forward lunge. The other stretches are recommended, though not required.

Wall Push-Up

1 Place your hands on a wall about shoulder-width apart and position your feet as far away from the wall as you feel comfortable. The farther your feet are from the wall, the harder the move will become. Engage your core to keep your back straight and your body in a straight line from head to feet; don't lean your head forward.

2 Inhale as you lower your entire body toward the wall, stopping before your head touches.

Exhale and, using your chest and arms, push your body away from the wall back to starting position.

Forward Lunge

1 Stand tall with your feet shoulder-width apart and your arms hanging at your sides.

2 Take a large step forward with your right foot, bend both knees and drop your hips straight down until both knees are bent 90 degrees. Your left knee should almost be touching the ground and your left heel should be off the ground. Keep your core engaged and your back, neck and hips straight at all times during this movement.

Pushing up with your right leg, straighten both knees and return to starting position. Repeat with the other leg.

REVERSE VARIATION: Reverse lunges are just like their forward counterparts, but begin by taking a step backward. These can make it slightly more difficult to maintain your balance and are a bit better for activating supporting muscles in your pelvis, legs and core.

Recommended Stretches

Standing Hamstring Stretch

THE STRETCH: Stand with both feet together. Step your left foot forward 10 to 12 inches in front of your right foot with your heel on the floor and your toes lifted. With your abdominals engaged, bend your right knee slightly and lean forward from your hips, not your back or shoulders. You may need to rotate the toes of your right foot slightly outward to maintain balance and get a deep stretch. Keeping your shoulders back (don't round them to get a deeper stretch), place both hands on your left leg at the thigh and hold for 15–30 seconds.

Switch sides.

TIP: Don't place your hands on your knee as the additional force can cause damage by hyperextending the joint.

Behind-the-Head Shoulder Stretch

THE STRETCH: Stand with your feet shoulder-width apart. Maintaining a straight back, grab your elbows with the opposite hand. Slowly raise your arms until they're slightly behind your head. Keeping your right hand on your left elbow, drop your left hand to the top of your right shoulder blade. Gently push your left elbow down with your right hand, and hold for 10 seconds.

Rest for 10 seconds and then repeat with opposite arms.

Standing Quadriceps Stretch

THE STRETCH: Stand with your feet hip-width apart. Bend your left leg and bring your left foot towards the bottom of your left buttock. Grasp your foot with your right hand, using your left hand to balance against a wall, desk or chair. With your knee pointed directly at the floor, gently pull your foot toward your butt until you find a position that stretches the front of your thigh. Hold that position for 15–30 seconds.

Switch sides.

Additional Exercises

Jumping rope is an extremely efficient exercise for shredding your body while building endurance and flexibility. In order to create a well-balanced training program for total-body fitness, we've added some plyometric moves to build explosive power in your legs and a dozen quality core-strengthening exercises. The Prep, Basic and Advanced programs are designed for maximum fat burning using high-intensity supersets that'll have you working your entire body through a full range of motion.

Bodyweight strength training combined with cardiovascular exercises are the most efficient way to build strength and develop a lean ripped physique. Let's be honest, though—none of us are perfect. Due to years of improper posture, sports injuries or even weak musculature, we all have imbalances that can affect proper form and even put us on the fast track to injury. In addition, jumping into a new exercise routine too quickly or doing the exercises with improper form can exacerbate any pre-existing injury.

It's very important that you focus on proper form and utilize the proper muscles to complete each exercise. Read the exercise descriptions, study the photos and take each movement as slowly as possible to make sure you're executing each properly. Now's the time to fix your form—it becomes increasingly more difficult as time goes on and you've been performing the exercises improperly. Always listen to your body. Take it easy and be smart about determining what's normal soreness from a workout and what's a nagging injury that you're aggravating. If you think it's the latter, take a few extra days off and see if the soreness passes. If you have any previous injuries or lingering pain and soreness persists, please see a medical professional.

You should expect to experience mild soreness and fatigue, especially when you're just getting started. The feeling of your muscles being "pumped" and the fatigue of an exhausting workout should be expected. These are positive feelings.

On the other hand, any sharp pain, muscle spasm or numbness is a warning sign that you need to stop and not push yourself any harder. Some small muscle groups may fatigue faster because they're often overlooked in other workouts.

Side Hop

This great agility drill uses fast-twitch muscle fibers and a whole bunch of stabilizing muscles. You'll still be jumping over the rope, but now it'll be lying on the ground.

1 Place the jump rope on the floor and stretch it out to form a straight line. Stand parallel to the rope so it's about 10 inches away from your right foot. Bend your knees, crouch at your waist and swing your arms down by your sides and prepare to jump over the rope.

2 – 3 Leaning slightly to the right, extend your legs forcefully and jump to your right as high as you can and land with your left foot approximately 10 inches to the right of the rope. Bend your knees and land softy on the balls of your feet in a controlled manner.

Immediately after landing, bend your knees, crouch at your waist and swing your arms down by your sides and jump over the rope to your left, landing with your right foot approximately 10 inches to the left of the rope. That's 1 rep.

Forward Jump

Just like the Side Hop, this exercise is performed with you jumping over the rope; the difference is that this version is more of a power movement. You'll be performing a deep squat and jumping forward using the explosive extension of your calves and quads and the extension of your hamstrings, glutes and hip flexors.

1 Place the jump rope on the floor and stretch it out to form a straight line. Stand perpendicular to the rope so it's about 12 inches away from your toes. Bend deeply at your knees, crouch at your waist and swing your arms down by your sides as you prepare to jump forward over the rope.

2 From a squatting position with your weight shifted forward to the balls of your feet, straighten your legs and explode forward and upward, jumping over the rope and as far forward as possible.

3 Land softly by bending your knees to absorb the impact as your feet hit the floor. Rise up to a standing position and walk back to starting position.

That's 1 rep.

Squat Jump

1 Stand tall with your feet shoulder-width apart and toes pointed slightly outward, about 11 and 1 o'clock. Extend your arms along both sides with your palms facing your hips. Bend at your hips and knees and "sit back" just a little bit as if you were about to sit directly down into a chair. Keep your head up, eyes forward and arms extended so your hands nearly touch the floor. As you descend, contract your glutes while your body leans forward slightly so that your shoulders are almost in line with your knees. Your knees should not extend past your toes and your weight should be slightly forward of a normal squat—between the middle of your foot and forefoot. Stop when your knees are at 90 degrees and your thighs are parallel to the floor.

2 In a rapid motion, straighten your legs and jump straight up while you push off of the balls of your feet in an attempt to jump as high as you can. Swing your hands directly overhead while extending your arms to reach as high as possible.

With your knees bent, land in a controlled manner and continue your downward momentum to prepare for the next repetition.

That's 1 rep.

Reverse Crunch

How do you get all the core-strengthening benefits of a crunch with very limited stress on the lower back? Reverse crunches are the answer! Keep your back straight and lower legs on a level plane throughout this slow and controlled movement.

1 Lie flat on your back with your legs extended along the floor and your arms along your sides, palms down.

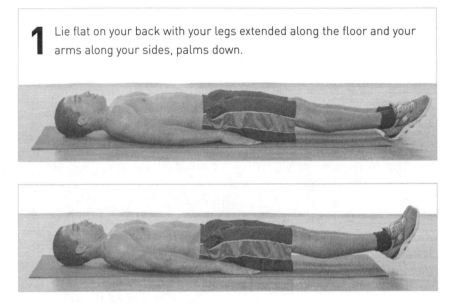

2 Contracting your lower abdominal muscles, lift your feet 4 to 6 inches off the floor, bend your knees and bring them in toward your chest. Be careful not to put excessive pressure on your lower back by bringing your hips off the floor. Pause when your glutes rise slightly off the mat.

3 Extend your legs and lower them until your feet are 4 to 6 inches off the floor.

Wood Chop

1 Stand tall with your feet shoulder-width apart, holding a medicine ball in front of you.

2 Lower your body into a squat until your knees are bent 90 degrees, and bring the ball down to touch your right foot.

3 Stand tall, twisting your torso to the left and lifting your arms straight up over your head. Your right shoulder should be in front and you should be looking to the left.

Repeat to the other side.

Cobra

1 Lying on your stomach, place your hands directly under your shoulders with your fingers facing forward. Straighten your legs and point your toes.

2 Exhale and engage your core while lifting your chest off the floor and pushing your hips gently into the floor. Your arms help guide you through the movement, and your elbows should remain slightly bent at the top of the extension; your hips should remain in contact with the mat. Hold the "up" position for 3–5 seconds, then gently roll your upper body back to the floor.

STRETCH VARIATION: When performing this as a stretch, hold the "up" position for 15–30 seconds, and then rest for 10 seconds.

Hip Raise

This exercise is a slow and controlled motion that works the entire core—back, hips and abs—and provides a great way to work those muscles without any impact. The starting position is the same as that of a sit-up.

1 Lie on your back with your knees bent to about 90 degrees and feet flat on the floor. Extend your hands toward your hips and place your arms and palms flat on the floor at your sides.

2 Engage your abdominal muscles to keep your core tight, and exhale while you press your feet into the floor and raise your hips and lower back up, forming a straight line from your sternum to your knees. Do not push your hips too high or arch your back. Hold this position for 15–30 seconds, and then inhale and slowly return to starting position.

That's 1 rep.

VARIATION: To work your core and stabilizers even more, when your hips reach the top of the motion and your body is flat from sternum to knees, raise one foot off the floor and extend it in front of you in the same line as your torso. Alternate legs with each repetition.

Bird Dog

The Bird Dog is an excellent exercise for developing abdominal and hip strength and flexibility, and also for working your lower back by stabilizing your spine throughout the movement.

1 Get on your hands and knees with your legs bent 90 degrees, knees under your hips, toes on the floor and your hands on the floor directly below your shoulders. Keep your head and spine neutral; do not let your head lift or sag. Contract your abdominal muscles to prevent your back from sagging; keep your back flat from shoulders to butt for the entire exercise.

2 In one slow and controlled motion, simultaneously raise your left leg and right arm until they're on the same flat plane as your back. Your leg should be parallel to the ground, not raised above your hip; your arm should extend directly out from your shoulder and your biceps should be level with your ear. Hold this position for 3–5 seconds and then slowly lower your arm and leg back to starting position.

That's 1 rep. Repeat on the other side.

Leg Lift

These are commonly called scissors or flutter kicks, and are a great way to isolate your abs.

1 Lie flat on your back with your legs extended along the floor and your arms along your sides, palms down. Contract your lower abdominal muscles and lift your feet 6 inches off the floor. Hold for 3 seconds.

2 While keeping your left foot in place, lift your right foot 6 inches higher (it should now be 12 inches off the floor). Hold for 3 seconds.

3 Simultaneously lower your right leg back to 6 inches off the floor while raising your left foot 6 inches higher. Hold for 3 seconds.

   This counts as 2 reps.

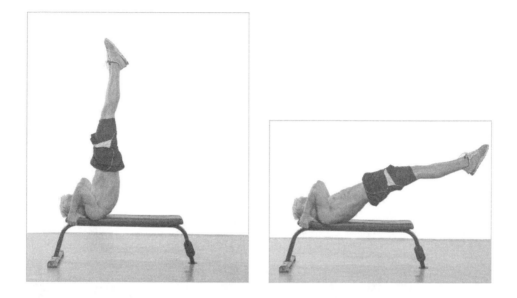

ADVANCED VARIATION: Lying on your back on a flat or incline bench, reach behind your head and grasp the bench with both hands. Exhale, engage your core and straighten your body from sternum to toes. Raise your entire body as one piece while leaving your shoulder blades in contact with the bench. Maintain a straight line with your lower back, hips and legs throughout the entire movement, and stop at the top when you can no longer keep your body on a flat plane. Lower slowly toward the bench and pause before your glutes or back touches. That's 1 rep.

Marching Twist

This high-intensity move works your obliques, hips and abs and gets your heart rate up.

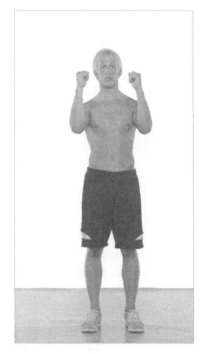  

1 Stand tall with your feet shoulder-width apart. Bring your arms in front of you and bend your elbows 90 degrees.

2 Twist your torso to the right and raise your left knee to your right elbow.

3 Repeat with your right knee and left elbow. A little hop with the bottom foot helps you keep your momentum going from leg to leg.

Superman

Interestingly enough, this exercise is not performed "up, up and away" but actually on your stomach, flat on the ground. However, the Man of Steel would greatly appreciate the importance of this move as it strengthens your lower back and gives some due attention to your erector spinae—you know, those muscles that keep you vertical.

1 Lying face down on your stomach, extend your arms directly out in front of you and your legs behind you. Keep your knees straight as if you were flying.

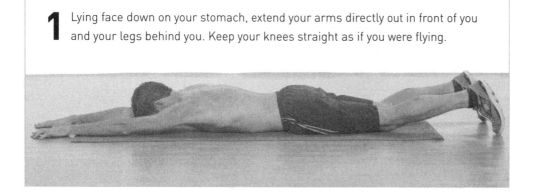

2 In a slow and controlled manner, contract your erector spinae and reach your arms forward and legs backward toward opposite walls, and allow your arms and feet to raise 3 to 5 inches off the floor. Your head should maintain a straight position with your spine; don't arch your back. This move is as much of a "stretch" as it is an exercise. Hold for 5 seconds.

Lower slowly back to starting position.

Mountain Climbers

1 Assume the top position of a push-up with your hands directly under your shoulders and toes on the ground. Keep your core engaged and your body in a straight line from head to feet.

2 Lift your right toe slightly off the ground, bring your right knee to your chest and place your right foot on the ground under your body.

3 With a very small hop from both toes, extend your right foot back to starting position and at the same time bring your left knee to your chest and place your left foot on the ground under your body.

Continue switching, making sure to keep your hips low.

Mason Twist

This exercise works the oblique abdominal muscles, the erector spinae and even the hip flexors. Always be careful when using weights in a twisting motion as you can easily injure your lower back. Start with the lightest possible weight and work your way up as you become more comfortable with the move and refine your form.

1 Sit on the floor with your knees comfortably bent, feet on the floor, arms bent 90 degrees and hands holding a medicine ball or weight in front of your chest. Lift your feet 4 to 6 inches off the floor and balance your body weight on your posterior. Keep your core tight to protect your back.

2 While maintaining the same hip position, twist your entire torso at the waist and touch the ball to the floor on the left side of your body.

3 Rotate back to center, keeping your feet off the floor and maintaining your balance using the supporting core muscles. Then rotate to your right and touch the ball to the floor.

Return to center. That's 1 rep.

Inchworm

This great full-body exercise is a perfect test for hamstring and lower back flexibility. In this motion-based exercise, you'll advance forward approximately 4 feet per repetition, so plan your exercise positioning accordingly.

1 Stand with your feet about hip-width apart and fold over so that your hands touch the floor.

2 – 3 Keeping your hands firmly on the floor to balance your weight, walk your hands out in front of you one at a time until you're at the top of a push-up. Hold for 3 seconds.

4 – 5 Keeping your hands firmly on the floor to balance your weight, "walk" your feet toward your head by taking very small steps on your toes. Imagine that your lower legs are bound together and you can only bend your feet at each ankle. As you continue walking your feet toward your head, your butt will rise and your body will form an inverse "V." When you've stretched your hamstrings, glutes and calves as far as you can, hold that position for 3 seconds. That's 1 rep.

Bicycle Crunch

Rated by the American Council on Exercise as the number-one way to target the rectus abdominis, this move gets your whole body in motion and really works the entire core.

1 Lie flat on your back with your legs extended straight along the floor and your hands at both sides of your head, fingers touching your temples.

2 Raise your feet 6 inches off the floor while simultaneously contracting your rectus abdominis and lifting your upper back and shoulders off the floor. In one movement, bend your left knee and raise your left leg so that the thigh and shin are at 90 degrees; rotate your torso using your oblique muscles so that your right elbow touches the inside of your left knee.

3 Rotate your torso back to center and lower your upper body toward the floor, stopping before your shoulders touch. Extend your left knee and return your foot to 6 inches off the floor and bend your right leg to 90 degrees. Contract your abs, rotate and touch your left elbow to your right knee. That's 2 reps.

Index

Acknowledgments

Thank you to Chad Taylor, Mary Gines and Austin Akre for their hard work delivering great, detailed jump rope photos for this book. Special thanks to Skechers GoRun, Body Glide, and Ben Sturner at Leverage Agency for their passion and support of 7 Weeks to Fitness. Without the love and support from Kristen, my family and friends, this book would not have been possible.

—Brett

Thank you to my mother, Sandra Warner, for instilling in me the love of fitness and healthy living. Special thanks to Brett Stewart, my coauthor and friend, for being there through the years on our fitness journey.

—Jason

About the Authors

Brett Stewart is an NCCPT Personal Trainer, ultra-marathoner and avid triathlete living in Phoenix, Arizona. A founding member of the ESPN Triathlon Team, his love for competition and new challenges is second only to his joy for introducing people to sports and fitness. Brett is the author of *7 Weeks to 50 Pull-Ups*, *7 Weeks to Getting Ripped* and *7 Weeks to 300 Sit-Ups*, and can be found online at www.7weekstofitness.com.

Jason Warner is an ISSA Certified Strength Trainer, fitness and sports enthusiast, ultra-marathoner, triathlete, CrossFitter and overall Olympic lifting nut. He currently lives in Adelaide, South Australia, with his wife and two young children. Jason contributed to *7 Weeks to 50 Pull-Ups* and *7 Weeks to Getting Ripped*, and can be found online at www.7weekstofitness.com and athgeek.com.